Creative Imagery

Discoveries and Inventions
in Visualization

D1544171

Creative Imagery
Discoveries and Inventions
in Visualization

Ronald Finke
Texas A & M University

LEA

1990

LAWRENCE ERLBAUM ASSOCIATES, PUBLISHERS

Hillsdale, New Jersey

Hove and London

Lawrence Erlbaum Associates, Inc., Publishers
365 Broadway
Hillsdale, New Jersey 07642

Library of Congress Cataloging-in-Publication Data

Finke, Ronald A.
    Creative imagery: discoveries and inventions in visualization/
by Ronald Finke.
        p. cm.
    Includes bibliographical references and index.
    ISBN 0-8058-0772-1
    1. Creative ability. 2. Visualization. 3. Imagery (Psychology)
4. Creative abiilty in science. I. Title.
    BF408.F45   1990
    153.3'2—dc20   90-3556
                                                          CIP

Printed in the United States of America
10 9 8 7 6 5 4 3 2

Contents

Acknowledgments

I would like to thank my students and colleagues for their many contributions to the ideas and experiments presented in this book: Janet Davidson, Martha Farah, Jennifer Freyd, Howard Kurtzman, Laura Lekich, Marvin Levine, Donna Mc-Keown, Steven Pinker, Larry Parsons, Linda Radin, Traci Ratliff, Jonathan Schooler, Gary Shyi, Karen Slayton, Steven Smith, Linda Wagner, and Tom Ward.

I would like to thank, in particular, Chad Neff, whose discussions on creativity, art, and aesthetics stimulated many of the ideas on creative invention that I have attempted to present here for the first time.

Portions of the author's research were supported by Grant 5R01MH-3980903 from the National Institute of Mental Health.

Chapter

1

Introduction

Every person has the potential to make creative discoveries in their imagery. Moreover, it is possible to demonstrate this experimentally for many types of creative discoveries. The experiments I report will show, in fact, that certain techniques are remarkably effective in stimulating the discovery of unexpected patterns, new inventions, and creative concepts—all within imagination. And these are techniques that anyone can learn to use.

A unique feature of this book is that it combines the experimental method and creative exploration. Most experimental studies on imagination constrain how the images are to be formed (e.g., Finke, 1989; Kosslyn, 1980; Shepard & Cooper, 1982). In contrast, previous books on how to engage in creative visualization have not been extensively based on experimental techniques (e.g., Adams, 1974; Arnheim, 1969; Edwards, 1986; McKim, 1980). This book attempts to do both.

I begin by considering examples of famous anecdotes in which mental images evidently led to creative insights and discoveries.

ANECDOTES OF CREATIVE DISCOVERIES IN IMAGERY

Roger Shepard (1978, 1988) has compiled a remarkable collection of anecdotes, mostly from eminent scientists and mathematicians, regarding the use of mental imagery in scientific and conceptual discovery. The interesting feature of these accounts is how the insights often arose spontaneously, as one considered the implications of the visualized forms and structures. These insights were typically

1

surprising, in much the same way that a person might be surprised upon finding the missing clue to a mystery. In these cases of image discovery, however, the "clues" were evidently generated from within the human mind itself.

Perhaps the most famous anecdote concerning the use of imagery in scientific discovery is that of Kekulé, who discovered the molecular structure of benzene. In his own account, Kekulé described having dreamed of a snake coiled in a circle, biting its own tail. Kekulé had been considering the problem of the underlying structure of organic molecules. He then suddenly realized that the snake's position in his image represented the key molecular structure he had been searching for.

Similarly, Einstein reported having been led to many of his fundamental insights by doing thought experiments in imagination. For example, by visualizing how the world would look if one were to travel beside a beam of light, he was led to the concept of special relativity. His accounts of having engaged in "combinational play" in imagery, as the preferred method for thinking about problems, again suggests that imagery can provide an internal medium for invention and discovery.

Shepard considered reports of many other examples among famous scientists of the use of visualization in moments of creative insight, notably those of James Clerk Maxwell, Michael Faraday, Sir Francis Galton, James Watt, Nicola Tesla, and, among recent physicists, Richard Feynman, Stephen Hawking, and Mitchell Feigenbaum. There have also been accounts of the use of creative visualization in various technological advances. For instance, Ferguson (1977) brought together numerous examples of mechanical inventions that were inspired by creative mental imagery. It seems, in fact, as if most of the important insights in the physical and applied sciences have come from visual images of some kind.

In a recent critique, Weisberg (1986) questioned whether accounts such as those of Kekulé actually occurred in the way they were reported. For example, there are indications that Kekulé's insight did not actually occur in a nocturnal dream, but rather, in a daydream. Weisberg also questioned the purported "leaps of insight" in many of these accounts. For purposes of the present investigations, such considerations are largely irrelevant. The key focus here is on the conditions that give rise to creative insights in imagery, and not the particular kind of imagery that is used, or exactly how the insights occur.

A NEW APPROACH TO CREATIVE INSIGHT AND INVENTION

The central idea I shall develop in this book is that creative discoveries and inventions might best be achieved by taking what most people would regard as a very indirect approach. Instead of starting out by thinking of what kinds of inventions are needed, or what new ideas are feasible, one conceives of a general object or shape that is intuitively interesting or appealing, and then considers its possible uses, as the situation demands. This is in the spirit of general recommendations for nondirective thinking that have been made by previous writers on creativity and problem solving (e.g., de Bono, 1967; Hayes, 1981; Levine, 1987).

The realization of a new idea or invention is thus largely unanticipated; it follows from the structure of the imagined form. However, it doesn't *necessarily* follow from any particular form, in that many other creative interpretations might have been possible, given other problems and considerations that might have been present at the time. In other words, there are many possible discoveries that the same imagined form can inspire, depending on what is desired or required. This will become clearer once the experiments on creative invention are presented. For the moment, an analogy might help.

Imagine a person stranded on a deserted island, who, out of boredom, considers interesting combinations of the small number of raw materials that he or she finds—and then realizes that some of these fanciful constructions have unexpected, practical applications. The person didn't begin by trying to assemble the raw materials to make something that had a specific function or purpose; rather, the inventive insights followed the person's "combinational play."

The basic notion here is that real creativity comes from using the things we create, not creating the things we use. The idea is similar to that found in modern "free writing" approaches to composition, where one starts out by generating many sentences and possible ideas, and then selects the ones that begin to make sense, and which then lead to new insights and understandings (e.g., Elbow, 1981).

I propose that one should consider turning the inventive process "inward," generating and exploring mental images that I call "preinventive forms." These forms are the products of the combinational play of visualization; they need not be structured according to a particular problem or task. In fact, it's better not to try to do so. Creative insights follow naturally as one explores possible interpretations of the preinventive forms. Typically, one ends up inventing things that one never previously considered, or discovering solutions to problems that one was not trying to solve. On the contrary, it is more likely to be a coincidence when a preinventive form leads you to discover something specific that you were trying to discover.

As I will argue later on, I don't believe that these instances of "image discoveries" are the products of unconscious processes or the like (e.g., Erdelyi, 1974; Marcel, 1983). Rather, I believe they are mostly accidental discoveries, in that the same imagined form could be interpreted as many different kinds of inventions or concepts—depending on what the person happened to be thinking about. Indeed, many of the inventions I will describe give one the impression that they could not have been conceived of as anything else, yet this is an illusion. Great insight may simply be the result of interpreting visualized structures that are inherently meaningful only in a very general sense.

COMPONENTS OF CREATIVITY

Throughout this book, "creative" discoveries are defined according to two separate dimensions—one being the *practicality* of an invention (or the *sensibility* of a concept), and the other its *originality*. Admittedly, there are other dimensions of creativity that one might consider (e.g., see Sternberg, 1988); moreover, there is a sense in which something can be regarded as "creative" without being practical. Nevertheless, the definition will prove useful in evaluating the quality of inventions and concepts that the present methods inspire.

SCOPE OF THIS BOOK

The various findings reported here are based on a total of 18 experiments, 9 of which were devoted specifically to discovering creative inventions in imagery. These studies, which were conducted over the past 3 years, involved more than 800 subjects participating in over 5,000 experimental trials. Hundreds of creative inventions resulted, and many of these are described in the text. In addition, the chapters present these findings in their actual chronological order, so that readers can consider how the ideas and experimental methods evolved across the individual studies.

There are certain aspects of creativity that are not considered in this book. First, I do not discuss the very large literature on problem solving, although I do consider the implications of the present findings for general strategies for how to go about solving problems. For reviews of the problem solving literature, the reader is referred to the following sources: Hayes (1981), Levine (1987), Newell and Simon (1972), Polya (1957), and Wickelgren (1974).

Also, individual differences are not considered to any great extent. There is already an enormous literature on individual differences in creativity and visual cognition that the reader may wish to consult (e.g., Cooper, 1976b; Cooper & Regan, 1982; Davidson, 1986; Kosslyn, Brunn, Cave, & Wallach, 1984; Marks, 1973; Slee, 1980; Sternberg, 1977, 1988; Torrance, 1974). This is not because I am uninterested in individual differences; rather, my primary concern has been to develop techniques for creative invention that virtually anyone can learn to use.

READER PARTICIPATION

Readers will be able to use the various methods I describe for making their own creative discoveries. In each of the following chapters, I have created opportunities to participate in the actual experimental tasks. If they are like many of the subjects in these experiments—who were undergraduate students without any prior training—readers should be able to use these techniques to considerable success. In fact, in the most successful of these experiments, almost two-thirds of the subjects were able to generate at least one creative invention in six attempts, under extremely limited time constraints! These are, I believe, learnable skills that one can apply across many conceptual domains.

Not only are the techniques described here useful in coming up with new inventions for practical devices, they are also useful in coming up with new conceptual ideas or principles, as I will describe near the end of the book. Readers will be given an opportunity to extend the techniques in this way as well.

Subjects in these experiments not only claimed to be excited about their discoveries, they also reported that they intended to develop their ideas further. Some have even asked me whether they might be able to patent their ideas! I cannot promise that all of the inventions and concepts that these methods will inspire are going to be truly novel, having never been thought of by anyone else before. This, however, is a secondary issue. The crucial thing is whether the methods enable people to make discoveries that they might not have made otherwise, and which lead them to new realizations and insights. Ultimately, I will leave it to readers to judge this for themselves.

The next two chapters report the findings of background research and describe the various kinds of control procedures that were included to rule out alternative explanations. These chapters will be of particular interest to readers who might be concerned about methodological issues in imagery experiments. Although all readers may find it interesting to try out examples of these earlier tasks, those who are interested primarily in learning to use the creative invention techniques may wish to begin with Chapter 4.

Chapter

2

Visual Discoveries in Imagery

Before one can make creative discoveries in imagery, it must be possible to recognize meaningful shapes or patterns that "emerge" when images are formed. These emergent shapes and patterns, moreover, should not be so obvious that one could easily anticipate them. They should, instead, lead to genuine visual discoveries, often to the surprise of the person forming the image. For this reason, this chapter emphasizes control procedures that have been included in imagery studies of this type.

THE NEED FOR EXPERIMENTAL VERIFICATION

The reason it is necessary to demonstrate that images can have emergent properties is that people often find it difficult to detect "hidden" patterns in their images. As one example, Reed (1974) reported an experiment showing that, when asked to form mental images of patterns made up of line drawings of simple forms and geometric shapes, people often fail to recognize nonobvious parts of the patterns. Consider, for example, the pattern shown in Fig. 2.1, consisting of a juxtaposed pair of "Roman numeral 10" symbols. Subjects in the experiment were allowed to inspect the pattern briefly before it was removed. They were then shown drawings of possible parts of the pattern and were asked whether the parts had been contained in the original pattern, much like the way a "hidden" figure can appear in a drawing. Reed found that the subjects could rarely detect those parts that would not have been obvious initially when the original patterns had been inspected.

For example, cover the pattern in Fig. 2.1 and try visualizing it. Does the

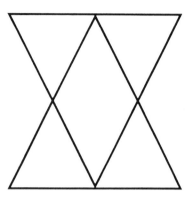

FIG. 2.1. Example of patterns used to explore people's ability to detect "hidden" forms in mental images. (From Reed, 1974, from *Memory & Cognition*, Vol. 2, pp. 329–336, reprinted by permission of Psychonomic Society, Inc.)

pattern contain a triangle? A diamond? What about a parallelogram? Most people find it easy to detect the four triangles and the diamond in their image, but difficult to detect the parallelogram. However, by removing the cover and inspecting the pattern, it is now relatively easy to find a parallelogram— in fact, there are two of them. Reed concluded, therefore, that people may not be able to detect parts of patterns in images that would have gone unnoticed at the time the images were formed. Because these "hidden" parts would not have been included in a normal description of the pattern, they would not have been represented in the image, and hence, would not have been detected.

In the same spirit, Chambers and Reisberg (1985) reported that people find it difficult to experience spontaneous "reversals" of perceptually ambiguous figures in imagery. For instance, consider the famous "Necker cube," shown in Fig. 2.2. As you continue to observe this figure, it appears to reverse in depth—first one face of the cube appears closer, then the other. Chambers and Reisberg reported that people do not experience reversals of the Necker cube in imagery, nor do they experience perceptual reversals of other similar kinds of ambiguous figures.

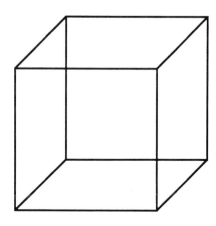

FIG. 2.2. Example of the "Necker cube," a perceptually ambiguous figure that appears to reverse in depth as one continues to inspect it. Such patterns do not exhibit spontaneous reversals in imagery.

They concluded that it may not be possible to reinterpret an image once it is tied to some initial interpretation. (For additional examples of perceptually ambiguous figures, see Attneave, 1971).

THE EMPIRICAL CHALLENGE

My interest in exploring creative visualization began with a concern over how to demonstrate that it was, in fact, possible to detect novel patterns in an image and to reinterpret an image in unexpected ways. My colleagues and I had often had the experience of detecting new perceptual relations in an image, and of reinterpreting an image in ways that seemed quite unrelated to the initial meaning of the image. It was therefore puzzling why the studies just mentioned failed to find evidence for emergent patterns in imagery or of image reinterpretation.

A possible explanation was suggested by a series of studies carried out by Stephen Kosslyn and his students. They found that mental images are generated by assembling the parts of the image one part at a time, and that the parts represent meaningful "chunks" or "units" in the imagined object or pattern (Kosslyn, Cave, Provost, & von Gierke, in press; Kosslyn, Reiser, Farah, & Fliegel, 1983). In addition, they found that when an image fades, it does so one part at a time, again with the parts representing meaningful chunks or units. These effects are more pronounced whenever the image corresponds to a complex pattern consisting of many parts, in which case one is constantly having to regenerate the faded parts in order to maintain the image (e.g., Kosslyn, 1975, 1980).

This might explain, first of all, the difficulty people had in detecting, entirely within imagination, the hidden figures studied by Reed. If parts of an image fade as meaningful units based on an initial interpretation of the pattern, this might prevent one from detecting those parts that correspond to meaningful units based on some other interpretation. Similarly, the detection of perceptual reversals of ambiguous figures in imagery might be disrupted if meaningful parts of an image were continually fading and having to be regenerated, especially with relatively complex patterns such as the Necker cube. (Readers may verify these characteristics of a fading image by trying to maintain images of the patterns in Figs. 2.1 and 2.2.)

The challenge, therefore, was to come up with experimental tasks in which unexpected patterns would "emerge" in imagery, but where the image would be less susceptible to fading. I begin by describing a set of experiments conducted in collaboration with Steven Pinker and Martha Farah (Finke, Pinker, & Farah, 1989), which demonstrate that people *can* detect unexpected patterns when they visualize simple, familiar shapes and forms being combined and transformed in various ways. In presenting these findings, I will also give readers the opportunity to participate in the actual tasks.

IMAGINED COMBINATIONS
OF FAMILIAR PATTERNS

In our first experiment, 12 undergraduate students were asked to visualize patterns formed by combining pairs of familiar symbols and shapes, such as capital letters, numbers, and geometric forms. Verbal instructions were given for either superimposing or juxtaposing the two patterns; it was emphasized that the patterns should be aligned in the images so that edges or end points would always match up. The experimenter then asked the subjects to describe any new features or patterns they could detect while mentally "inspecting" their images. There were six trials per subject.

As a precaution against the possibility that extraneous visual cues might contaminate the results, the subjects always performed the task with their eyes closed. It was explained that the emergent patterns could correspond to simple geometric forms (e.g., a "square" or "triangle"), or to more complex symbols such as letters, numbers, or other familiar objects. The emergent patterns were then classified according to whether they constituted geometric or symbolic forms. To minimize the possibility of experimenter bias, which can sometimes be a problem in studies of this type (e.g., see Intons-Peterson, 1983; Orne, 1962; Rosenthal, 1976), a naive experimenter was used throughout the study; that is, one who was unaware of the predicted results.

To experience what this task was like, try imagining the capital letter "H". Now imagine superimposing the capital letter "X" directly over the "H", such that the four corners of each letter overlap. Can you now detect any new shapes or forms resulting from the superimposed letters?

When subjects in the study were actually given these instructions, they reported detecting geometric forms such as "right triangles," and symbolic forms such as "the letter M," a "butterfly," and a "bow-tie." Examples of patterns that were mentally combined in the experiment and the resulting pattern combinations are presented in Fig. 2.3. In all, across the 72 trials, subjects reported detecting a total of 120 geometric forms and 39 symbolic forms. In scoring these emergent forms, we adopted conservative conventions; only those forms were counted that would have resulted from mentally combining the two starting patterns, meaning that the forms could not have been present initially in either of the patterns alone.

When the subjects were interviewed at the conclusion of the experiment, they reported having been able to form a clear image on 86.1% of the trials. They also indicated that they were "surprised" by some of the patterns that they detected in their images; this reflected the "emergent" quality of the patterns. To verify that they had understood the instructions and had carried out the imagined constructions accurately, we also had them draw the patterns corresponding to their images at the end of each trial. These drawings revealed that they had combined the patterns correctly on 94.4% of the trials.

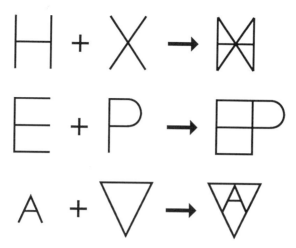

FIG. 2.3.   Examples of trial sequences used to explore the detection of emergent patterns in imagery, resulting when pairs of letters, numbers, or simple geometric forms were mentally superimposed. The first two patterns in each row were named, then subjects imagined combining them to make the patterns shown to the right of the arrows. They then reported any geometric or symbolic forms that they could "detect" by mentally "inspecting" the imagined, synthesized patterns. (From Finke, Pinker, and Farah, 1989, reprinted by permission.)

Thus, in contrast to the implications of Reed's study, we found that people can sometimes detect "hidden" patterns using imagery. However, we also found that people could detect more of these patterns—particularly, those corresponding to symbolic forms—when they inspected their drawings than when they simply relied on their images. In addition, few of the emergent forms would have constituted global reinterpretations of the entire pattern, in contrast to those studied by Chambers and Reisberg (1985).

There were, nevertheless, occasional reports of "global" emergent forms that were particularly striking. For example, for the "E" and "P" combination (see again Fig. 2.3), one subject reported detecting a "rotated grain silo." The relative scarcity of emergent patterns of this type, however, was a major limitation of our first experiment. Another limitation was that many of the emergent patterns, particularly those corresponding to geometric forms, might have been "deduced" from the individual features of the starting patterns. For example, for the superposition of the "H" and "X", one might have deduced that right triangles ought to appear, since the letter "H" has four right angles, which would be crossed by the diagonal lines in the letter "X". For these reasons, we conducted a second experiment to test specifically for the recognition of global, whole patterns resulting from the imagined constructions. And, we used procedures in which the emergent patterns would be better disguised.

EMERGENT PATTERNS FOLLOWING
IMAGINED TRANSFORMATIONS

A number of studies have shown that people are able to imagine rotations or other transformations of a pattern, in order to anticipate what the pattern would look like in a new position or orientation (e.g., Bundesen & Larsen, 1975; Cooper, 1976a; Corballis, 1988; Shepard & Cooper, 1982; Shepard & Metzler, 1971). For example, in a study by Lynn Cooper and Roger Shepard (1973), subjects had to say whether a rotated letter was normal or reflected (i.e., right-left reversed). The time it took them to do so increased as the letter was further rotated from its standard, upright position, suggesting that the subjects had imagined rotating the letter back to that position in order to judge its form. This process is commonly referred to as "mental rotation" (e.g., Shepard & Metzler, 1971).

Control studies have shown that mental rotations cannot easily be explained in terms of verbal or other analytical strategies that might have been based on the initial descriptions of a pattern. For example, the rate of mental rotation, at least for familiar or well-practiced patterns, does not depend on the visual complexity of the patterns (Bethell-Fox & Shepard, 1988; Cooper & Podgorny, 1976), implying that the mental rotations are performed on images as a whole, rather than on the separate parts of an image. Such findings suggested that it might be possible to recognize a pattern after it had been transformed extensively in imagination—even when the emergent pattern could not be deduced from the way the starting pattern initially appeared.

The technique that Pinker, Farah, and I used in our second experiment was to have subjects start out by imagining a single, familiar shape or pattern, such as a letter or number, and then to imagine transforming it in various ways according to a set of verbal instructions. At the conclusion of the transformation sequence, they were asked whether they could recognize the final pattern. As before, the entire procedure was conducted while the subjects kept their eyes closed. In addition, for each transformation sequence, there was always a specific "target" pattern that constituted a "correct" response. Subjects' drawings at the completion of each trial revealed how accurately they had carried out the transformations. There were again 12 subjects and a total of 72 trials.

The key feature of the procedure was that the transformation sequences were structured in such a way that the final patterns could not easily be deduced from the starting patterns. By using sequences of transformations that were unpredictable, we minimized the possibility that the subjects could anticipate, in advance, what the final patterns would be.

Here's an example of the task: Imagine the capital letter "B". Rotate it 90 degrees to the left, so that the curved lines are at the top. Put a triangle directly below it having the same width as the rotated "B" and pointing down. Remove the horizontal line. Can you recognize this pattern?

The sets of verbal instructions used for each of the six transformation sequences are given in Table 2.1. You may wish to try them out before reading on, to see

TABLE 2.1
Transformation Sequences Read to Subjects in Experiments
on Detecting Emergent Patterns

1. "Imagine the number '7'. Make the diagonal line vertical. Move the horizontal line down to the middle of the vertical line. Now rotate the figure 90 degrees to the left."

2. "Imagine the letter 'B'. Rotate it 90 degrees to the left. Put a triangle directly below it having the same width and pointing down. Remove the horizontal line."

3. "Imagine the letter 'Y'. Put a small circle at the bottom of it. Add a horizontal line halfway up. Now rotate the figure 180 degrees."

4. "Imagine the letter 'K'. Put a square next to it on the left side. Put a circle inside of the square. Now rotate the figure 90 degrees to the left."

5. "Imagine a 'plus'. Add a vertical line on the left side. Rotate the figure 90 degrees to the right. Now remove all lines to the left of the vertical line."

6. "Imagine the letter 'D'. Rotate it 90 degrees to the right. Put the number '4' above it. Now remove the horizontal segment of the '4' to the right of the vertical line."

Note: From Finke, Pinker, and Farah (1989). Reprinted by permission.

how many of the resulting patterns you could have recognized. The correct sequences and resulting patterns are given in Fig. 2.4.

We found, first of all, that the intended transformations were correctly performed on 59.7% of the trials. Of these, the subjects correctly identified the emergent pattern 58.1% of the time. These findings are presented in Table 2.2, according to how accurately the imagined transformations were carried out. Based on the subjects' drawings, we classified the transformations as correct (no errors), partially correct (with only a minor flaw or error), or incorrect. The subjects' responses were scored as correct (target pattern correctly identified), partially correct (a reported pattern which, although different from the target pattern, still constituted a legitimate interpretation), or incorrect (an interpretation that was not compatible with the final pattern). The table shows that correct performance on the task depended on how accurately the imagined transformation had been carried out. In particular, when the transformation had been incorrect, the subjects never identified the target patterns, whereas they did so on 63.8% of the trials when the transformation had been at least partially correct. This is important, because it helps to rule out the possibility that the target patterns could have been guessed simply on the basis of verbal descriptions of the starting patterns and the transformations.

ANTICIPATING THE EMERGENT PATTERNS

Still, it is possible that the target patterns could have been anticipated at some point prior to the final step in the transformation sequences, assuming that the transformations were performed correctly. That is, subjects might have inferred, from how the transformations were unfolding, what the intended target patterns

FIG. 2.4.   Depiction of correct transformation sequences used to explore the recognition of unexpected patterns in mental imagery, corresponding to the verbal descriptions given in Table 2.1. The correct resulting patterns, as shown above, were the letter "T", a heart, a stick figure,
a TV set, the letter "F", and a sailboat. (From Finke, Pinker, and Farah,
1989, reprinted by permission.)

were likely to be. To control for this possibility, Pinker, Farah, and I conducted
a third experiment, similar to the previous one, except that subjects were now
instructed to guess, at every point in the transformation sequence, what they
thought the final pattern would be. A new group of 12 subjects were used, and
there were a total of 72 trials.

For example, imagine the capital letter "F". Can you guess what the final
pattern will be? Now connect a lowercase letter "b" to the vertical line in the "F".

TABLE 2.2
Number of Emergent Patterns Identified According to the Accuracy
of the Imagined Transformations

	Accuracy of Transformation		
Pattern Identification	*Correct*	*Partially Correct*	*Incorrect*
Correct	25	2	0
Partially Correct	5	5	0
Incorrect	13	8	14

Note: The above classifications are based on a total of 72 trials. From Finke, Pinker, and Farah (1989). Reprinted by permission.

Can you guess the final pattern? Now flip the loop of the "b" around so that it's now on the left side of the vertical line. Can you now recognize this pattern?

The complete set of instructions for the six transformation sequences used in this experiment are presented in Table 2.3. The sequences were specifically designed such that the subjects would have difficulty identifying the final patterns until the very last step. Again, readers can try each of the sequences for themselves. Figure 2.5 presents the correct transformations and final patterns.

In Table 2.4, the number of correct guesses and final pattern identifications

TABLE 2.3
Transformation Sequences Read to Subjects in Experiments
on Guessing and Then Detecting Emergent Patterns

1. "Imagine a capital letter 'F'. (Guess #1). Connect a lowercase letter 'b' to the vertical line in the 'F'. (Guess #2). Now flip the loop of the 'b' around so that it's now on the left side of the vertical line." (Final Identification).

2. "Imagine a capital letter 'T'. (Guess #1). Rotate the figure 180 degrees. (Guess #2). Now add a triangle to the top of the figure, positioned so that its base is at the very top and it appears to be pointing down." (Final Identification).

3. "Imagine a lowercase letter 'k'. (Guess #1). Surround the letter with a circle. (Guess #2). Now remove the lower half of the letter, below the point where the lines intersect." (Final Identification).

4. "Imagine a capital letter 'N'. (Guess #1). Connect a diagonal line from the top right corner to the bottom left corner. (Guess #2). Now rotate the figure 90 degrees to the right." (Final Identification).

5. "Imagine a capital letter 'D'. (Guess #1). Rotate the figure 90 degrees to the left. (Guess #2). Now place a capital letter 'J' at the bottom." (Final Identification).

6. "Imagine a capital letter 'H'. (Guess #1). Rotate the figure 90 degrees to the right. (Guess #2). Now place a triangle at the top, with its base equal in width to that of the figure." (Final Identification).

Note: From Finke, Pinker, Farah (1989). Reprinted by permission.

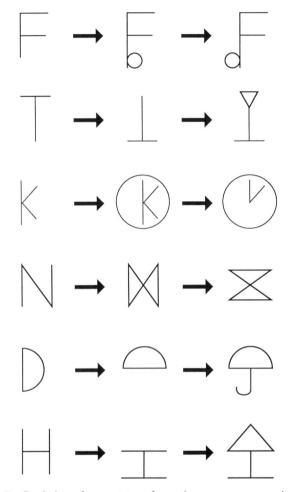

FIG. 2.5. Depiction of correct transformation sequences used to explore the guessing and eventual recognition of emergent patterns in mental imagery, corresponding to the verbal descriptions given in Table 2.3. The correct resulting patterns, as shown above, were a musical note, a yield sign (or wine glass), a clock face, an hourglass (or Roman numeral "10"), an umbrella, and a pine tree. (From Finke, Pinker, & Farah, 1989, reprinted by permission.)

are presented according to how accurately the subjects carried out the imagined transformations. When the transformations were performed accurately, which occurred on 66.7% of the trials, the final patterns were correctly recognized 47.9% of the time. In agreement with our previous experiment, as the accuracy of the imagined transformations decreased, the subjects were less likely to recognize the final patterns: When the transformations were classified as "partially

TABLE 2.4
Number of Correct Guesses and Final Pattern Identifications
According to the Accuracy of the Imagined Transformations

	Accuracy of Transformation		
	---	---	---
Type of Response	Correct	Partially Correct	Incorrect
Guess #1	0	0	0
Guess #2	2	1	0
Final Identification	21	3	1

Note: The above classifications are based on a total of 72 trials. From Finke, Pinker, and Farah (1989). Reprinted by permission.

correct," the final patterns were recognized 28.6% of the time, and when the transformations were classified as "wrong," they were recognized only 10% of the time.

The most significant result of this experiment, however, is that the final patterns were correctly guessed in advance on only 4.2% of the trials (see again Table 2.4). Thus, the subjects' ability to recognize the emergent patterns cannot be explained in terms of guessing strategies that might have been inspired by the nature of the transformations. Instead, the subjects reported that they were often surprised at having "detected" the final patterns—as readers may have experienced after having attempted these tasks.

EMERGENT PATTERNS IN THREE-DIMENSIONAL IMAGES

The possibility that emergent forms can also be recognized in imagined transformations of three-dimensional structures was explored in an earlier study by Pinker and Finke (1980). In this study, subjects were trained in remembering the exact positions of four small toys that were suspended at various heights inside a clear plexiglass cylinder. The objects were then removed, and the subjects were instructed to continue to imagine seeing the objects as the cylinder was rotated to a new, unexpected position. At this new position, they were asked to report what pattern was now "formed" by the relative positions of the four imagined toys, in much the same way that constellations of stars often form meaningful shapes and patterns.

Nearly half of the subjects (7 out of 16) reported "seeing" a tilted parallelogram in their images, and their subsequent drawings of the imagined configuration corresponded to close approximations of a parallelogram in every case. Yet, none of the subjects had been able to guess, before the cylinder was rotated, what the emergent pattern would be. Thus, as in the study by Finke, Pinker, and Farah, emergent patterns were recognized following an imagined transformation, even when they could not be anticipated.

SUMMARY

The findings presented in this chapter demonstrate that people can detect emergent patterns in imagery that were not anticipated at the time the image was initially formed. Controls for guessing show that most of these pattern recognitions are made only when people mentally "inspect" their images, whereupon they "discover" the patterns for the first time. These emergent pattern recognitions provide an empirical foundation for exploring creative discoveries in imagery, which is the topic of the next chapter.

THEORETICAL IMPLICATIONS

In contrast to the implications of earlier studies, these findings show that people are in fact capable of recognizing unexpected patterns that "emerge" as they construct and transform their images. As I have mentioned, this is a necessary condition for establishing that mental imagery can be used to make creative discoveries. For example, in order for someone to use imagery to recognize the possibilities of a creative invention, he or she must be able to recognize the significance of meaningful structures or patterns that emerge as the imagined object or form begins to take shape.

How is it possible that one can make visual discoveries in imagery? Pinker, Farah, and I proposed, as an explanation, that perceptual interpretive processes are applied to mental images in much the same way that they are applied to actual physical objects. In this sense, imagined objects can be "interpreted" much like physical objects. The interpretive processes may not be as efficiently applied in imagery as they are in perception, however, given the tendency for images to fade over time (e.g., see Pinker, 1984). The general notion that imagined objects and forms can often function in equivalent ways to real objects and forms has been supported by many previous studies (e.g., Farah, 1985; Finke, 1980, 1986a; Finke & Kurtzman, 1981; Podgorny & Shepard, 1978; Shepard, 1984; Shepard & Cooper, 1982).

A critic of these studies might argue that even though people claim to use imagery to make their discoveries, and report having "detected" meaningful patterns in their images, other kinds of cognitive processes might actually be responsible. For example, abstract, "propositional" knowledge structures and their associated processes might underlie performance on these tasks (e.g., Anderson, 1978; Pylyshyn, 1973, 1984). Propositional knowledge is nonverbal, and might govern one's performance even though one is not consciously aware of it. Hence, it cannot be ruled out by controls for simple guessing.

Throughout this book, my response to such criticisms is twofold: First, the past two decades of imagery research have shown that propositional theories simply cannot account for the vast majority of findings of imagery experiments, except in an unacceptably ad-hoc manner (e.g., Farah, 1988; Finke, 1989; Finke & Shepard, 1986; Kosslyn, 1975, 1976; Kosslyn & Pomerantz, 1977). In particular, the lawful manner in which images are scanned and transformed over time, as revealed by chronometric studies, places considerable strain on propositional theories (e.g., Cooper & Podgorny, 1976; Cooper & Shepard, 1984; Finke & Pinker, 1982; Kosslyn, Ball, & Reiser, 1978; Pinker, 1980; Shepard & Feng, 1972; Shepard & Metzler, 1971). Thus, although it may not be possible to rule out propositional accounts of imagery findings in every single case, I believe such accounts no longer present a serious challenge to imagery research. Rather, it is more important to control for potential artifacts in the procedures of the imagery experiments, such as experimenter bias.

My second response is quite simple. I claim that most of the imagery tasks I describe in this book are virtually impossible to do without using imagery, and I invite readers to verify this. From a practical standpoint, at least, the "reality" of these image discoveries can hardly be denied.

Chapter

3

Creative Mental Synthesis

Although the findings reviewed in the previous chapter indicate that people can make unexpected discoveries in their imagery, they do not reveal anything about the extent to which one might make *creative* discoveries in imagery. This is because the previous experiments restricted the manner in which images could be assembled and transformed. In the present chapter, I describe experiments demonstrating that people are also capable of making creative visual discoveries in their images, when constraints on the imagined constructions are removed.

PREVIOUS STUDIES ON MENTAL SYNTHESIS

Many previous studies have established that people can take the separate parts of a pattern and mentally assemble them, to verify, from memory, whether the assembled pattern matches a whole, presented pattern. For example, Glushko and Cooper (1978) gave subjects descriptions of how patterns composed of simple geometric parts were to be assembled, and then showed them drawings of test patterns, which they had to verify as matching the descriptions. They found that subjects no longer relied on the descriptions, but instead formed mental images, whenever they were given sufficient time to prepare for the test patterns. Chronometric measures confirmed this; when a 2-second preparation period was provided, the subjects' response times for verifying that the test patterns matched the described patterns was independent of the verbal complexity of the descriptions and the number of parts. These and other related findings (e.g., Klopfer, 1985; Nielsen & Smith, 1973; Thompson & Klatzky, 1978; Tversky, 1975) show that people can use imagery to mentally assemble the separately presented or described parts of a pattern, to verify that the completed pattern matches one that is actually presented.

These previous studies are limited, however, in two respects. First, they did not explore the possibility that people could recognize patterns that result from a mental synthesis when the "recognition" had to occur entirely within imagination—that is, in the absence of test patterns that could be used to verify the imagined forms. The studies considered in Chapter 2 demonstrate that this is indeed possible. Second, in these earlier studies on mental synthesis, subjects were always given explicit instructions for how to go about combining the parts— hence, they were not able to explore creative combinations of the parts. It is not enough merely to show that people can discover unexpected, emergent patterns in images when the procedures are specified; one must also show that people can make entirely new discoveries on their own, without being directed in how to do so. Otherwise, the visual discoveries, even if genuine, may be of no natural or practical consequence.

A PARADIGM FOR CREATIVE VISUALIZATION

Together with Karen Slayton, I developed a method for exploring the creative mental synthesis of randomly chosen forms (Finke & Slayton, 1988). In our initial experiment, 39 undergraduate students participated as subjects. The subjects were first shown the kinds of parts that might be used on each trial, which consisted of simple geometric shapes and alphanumeric characters, similar to the forms used by Finke, Pinker, and Farah (1989). The complete set of parts are presented in Fig. 3.1. Since the parts would be named at the beginning of the trials, the experimenter pointed out the specific names for each of the parts; these are provided in the figure caption.

The subjects were told that three of the parts would be named on each trial, and that they were to close their eyes and to try to mentally assemble the parts to make a recognizable figure. It was explained that the parts would be randomly selected each time, and that it was possible for the same part to occur twice or even three times on the same trial. They were to use all three parts in each of their imagined constructions.

The figures could be virtually anything—for example, letters, numbers, objects, familiar shapes and symbols—as long as the pattern was recognizable. The parts could vary in size, position, or orientation, and could be combined in any way, except that the parts could not be bent or otherwise altered in shape. However, the resulting figures had to correspond to something that could be easily named. If the subjects were able to come up with more than one recognizable figure, they were to select the best one.

The parts for each trial were randomly selected by a computer, with the only constraint being that the parts shown in the first two rows of Fig. 3.1 were three

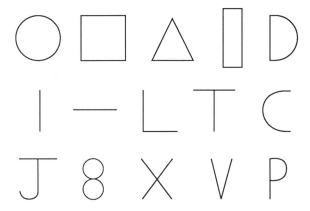

FIG. 3.1.   Parts used in experiments on creative mental synthesis. The parts were designated by the following names: CIRCLE, SQUARE, TRI-ANGLE, RECTANGLE, LETTER 'D', VERTICAL LINE, HORIZONTAL LINE, LETTER 'L', LETTER 'T', LETTER 'C', LETTER 'J', NUMBER '8', LETTER 'X', LETTER 'V', LETTER 'P'. Subjects in the experiment were to imagine combining three of the parts, which were randomly chosen, to make a recognizable shape or pattern. (From Finke & Slayton, 1988, *Memory & Cognition*, Vol. 16, pp. 252–257, reprinted by permission of Psychonomic Society, Inc.)

times as likely to be selected as those in the bottom row. This was done so that the more complex alphanumeric characters (such as the letters "J" and "P") would seldom comprise the entire set of all three parts. Using this selection procedure, there were 1,135 possible unique part combinations. The subjects were run in small groups of 4–6, with 8 trials per subject.

The remainder of the experimental procedure was as follows: After the subjects closed their eyes, and the names of the three parts were repeated, they were given 2 minutes to come up with a recognizable figure. At the end of the 2 minutes, the subjects opened their eyes and were instructed first to write down the name of the figure, if they came up with one, next to the appropriate trial number on a response sheet. They were then instructed to draw the figure on a separate response sheet. Once they began to draw the figure, they could not go back and change anything they wrote when naming it. This ensured that they were not simply recognizing the patterns for the first time in their drawings.

It is important to note that the subjects were never told to try to be original or creative; they were simply to come up with a recognizable pattern. Our hope was that the nature of the task itself would stimulate the exploration of creative combinations of the parts, since the parts were chosen arbitrarily and without regard to any particular "target" patterns. This seemed quite reasonable; given unusual sets of parts, one would almost have to think in original, creative ways to consider how the parts could be combined.

EXPERIMENTER PREDICTIONS
OF THE IMAGINED PATTERNS

As in the studies described in Chapter 2, we were careful to use a naive experimenter, to minimize the possibility that the subjects' performance might be influenced by the experimenter's awareness of the purpose of the study. In addition, as a further safeguard, we had the experimenter actually try to guess what figures subjects were most likely to come up with on every trial. The experimenter was given, in advance, the three parts that would be used on each trial, and was instructed to generate three guesses for each set of parts. Not only did this provide a conservative control for experimenter bias, it also provided a way of assessing whether the reported patterns might have been obviously suggested by the particular parts themselves.

The patterns were scored in the following way: Three judges independently rated how closely the names of the patterns corresponded to the drawings, using a 5-point scale, in which a rating of "5" meant "very good correspondence" and a rating of "1" meant "very poor correspondence." The judges were to assign a rating of "4" or "5" only if the drawing could be easily recognized from its name. Further, if the pattern was notably creative, and the correspondence rating was at least a "4", the judges were also to score the pattern as "creative." These ratings were not to be based on the quality of the drawings per se, but rather on whether the arrangements of parts depicted in the drawings would be recognized as the named figures had they been skillfully drawn—so that the subjects would not be penalized for lacking drawing skills.

The judges' ratings were then used to classify the patterns. If a pattern received an average correspondence rating of at least a "4", it was classified as a "recognizable" pattern. If a recognizable pattern was scored as "creative" by at least two of the judges, it was further classified as a "creative" pattern. These scoring conventions were thus conservative; "creative" patterns were counted as such only when they were also considered recognizable.

The actual number of recognizable and creative patterns, according to whether or not they were predicted by the experimenter, are presented in Table 3.1.

TABLE 3.1
Recognizable and Creative Patterns Reported by Subjects According
to Whether the Experimenter Correctly Predicted Them

Type of Pattern	Predicted	Not Predicted	Total
Recognizable	17	102	119
Creative	1	18	19

Note: The above classifications are based on a total of 312 trials. From Finke and Slayton (1988). From *Memory & Cognition,* Vol. 16, pp. 252–257, reprinted by permission of Psychonomic Society, Inc.

Overall, the subjects were able to come up with a recognizable pattern on 38.1% of the trials; of these, 19, or 16% were classified as creative patterns. As Table 3.1 also shows, the experimenter was able to guess only 14.3% of the recognizable patterns and only 1 of the 19 creative patterns, showing that these visual discoveries were not due simply to experimenter effects or were obviously implied by the sets of parts. Of the 39 subjects, 37 reported at least one recognizable pattern, and 12 reported at least one creative pattern.

Figure 3.2 presents four examples of recognizable patterns that were *not* judged as creative. In contrast, Fig. 3.3 presents four examples of creative patterns, consisting of a "bug," a "bowling ball," an "ice cream soda," and a "firecracker." There is something rather striking about these creative patterns; something, I believe, that goes beyond the personal impressions of the judges. Rather, I think most observers would agree that these mental constructions are indeed very clever and quite surprising.

Table 3.2 provides readers with the opportunity to experience the task for themselves. Ten sets of parts are provided; these were generated by a computer,

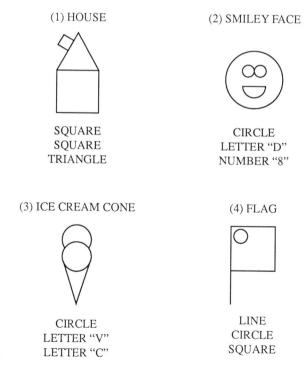

(1) HOUSE

SQUARE
SQUARE
TRIANGLE

(2) SMILEY FACE

CIRCLE
LETTER "D"
NUMBER "8"

(3) ICE CREAM CONE

CIRCLE
LETTER "V"
LETTER "C"

(4) FLAG

LINE
CIRCLE
SQUARE

FIG. 3.2.   Examples of recognizable patterns that were not classified as creative, together with the sets of parts that were used in the mental synthesis. (From Finke & Slayton, 1988, *Memory & Cognition*, Vol. 16, pp. 252–257, reprinted by permission of Psychonomic Society, Inc.)

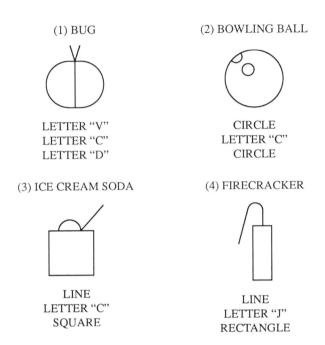

(1) BUG

LETTER "V"
LETTER "C"
LETTER "D"

(2) BOWLING BALL

CIRCLE
LETTER "C"
CIRCLE

(3) ICE CREAM SODA

LINE
LETTER "C"
SQUARE

(4) FIRECRACKER

LINE
LETTER "J"
RECTANGLE

FIG. 3.3. Examples of recognizable patterns that were classified as creative, together with the sets of parts that were used in the mental synthesis. Compare with the noncreative patterns shown in Fig. 3.2. (From Finke & Slayton, 1988, *Memory & Cognition*, Vol. 16, pp. 252–257, reprinted by permission of Psychonomic Society, Inc.)

TABLE 3.2
Examples of Sets of Parts Used in Experiments on Creative Mental Synthesis

1.	LETTER "L" LETTER "P" RECTANGLE		6.	LETTER "V" LETTER "D" LETTER "L"
2.	CIRCLE RECTANGLE LETTER "L"		7.	TRIANGLE LETTER "T" HORIZONTAL LINE
3.	LETTER "P" RECTANGLE LETTER "C"		8.	HORIZONTAL LINE LETTER "V" SQUARE
4.	VERTICAL LINE VERTICAL LINE RECTANGLE		9.	SQUARE TRIANGLE NUMBER "8"
5.	LETTER "L" TRIANGLE LETTER "D"		10.	RECTANGLE LETTER "D" LETTER "P"

and were not screened or preselected in any way. Hence they are representative of the kinds of trials that were used in the actual task. Read the names of the parts, then close your eyes and try to come up with a recognizable pattern. Remember that the parts can be combined in any way, and that you must use all three parts. Also, take note of the kinds of strategies that seem to work best.

At the end of the Finke and Slayton (1988) experiment, subjects filled out a simple questionnaire, reporting the most common strategy they had used for performing the task. This was included because the subjects were never told what particular strategy to use. Table 3.3 provides the four alternative choices that were given on the questionnaire. The overwhelming choice was the first alternative, which described a trial-and-error combining of the parts in an image until a familiar shape could be recognized. This was selected by nearly three-fourths of the subjects (74.4%), and accounted for 18 of the 19 creative patterns.

These reports correspond to our own subjective impressions for how the task can best be accomplished. At first, one might try thinking of particular objects or figures that could be associated with the individual parts, but this rarely leads to success. Rather, the most efficient strategy is to imagine combining the parts in various interesting ways and then mentally "seeing" if anything meaningful emerges—what Einstein had referred to as "combinational play" in his own thinking. As later chapters will show, this "combinational play" strategy is also remarkably successful when trying to discover creative inventions.

SUBJECT-GENERATED PREDICTIONS
OF THE PATTERNS

The fact that our experimenter rarely predicted the recognizable patterns does not necessarily mean that the subjects themselves could not have predicted them. Hence, we conducted a second experiment in which a new group of 70 subjects were given this opportunity. Prior to doing the experimental task, the subjects

TABLE 3.3
Post-Experimental Questionnaire Used to Assess the Most
Common Strategy for Generating Recognizable Patterns
in Creative Mental Synthesis

(1) "I tried combining the parts by trial and error in my image until I happened to recognize a familiar shape."

(2) "I first thought of a possible shape, and then tried to combine the parts in my image to see whether that particular shape could be made out of those parts."

(3) "I didn't form an image at all, but just thought about how the parts might be combined in a more abstract way."

(4) "I used some other strategy."

Note: From Finke and Slayton (1988). From *Memory & Cognition,* Vol. 16, pp. 252–257, reprinted by permission of Psychonomic Society, Inc.

were given sets of parts from half of the experimental trials, and were instructed to guess what patterns an experimental subject might come up with, given those particular parts. They were also given a complete description of the experimental task, although they were not to actually do the task when making their guesses.

They were encouraged to come up with as many as three guesses, and were given 30 seconds to do so—the time limit serving to reduce the likelihood that they would try imagining various combinations of the parts. Rather, we wanted their guesses to be based on their initial associations to the parts. They then participated in the experimental task, exactly as the previous subjects had done. They were told, in addition, that if they noticed that a set of parts was repeated from the guessing condition, they were to try to make one of the patterns they had guessed.

There were a total of 560 experimental trials in all. As shown in Table 3.4, for the 280 trials that were repeated from the guessing condition, a recognizable pattern was reported 44.3% of the time. Of these, 19, or 15.3%, were classified as highly creative, using the same criteria as before. Only 18.5% of the recognizable patterns were predicted by the subjects; this is statistically equivalent to the percent predicted by the experimenter (χ^2 (1) < 1). For the other 280 trials for which predictions were not made, recognizable patterns were reported on 39.3% of the trials, and there were 15 creative patterns. Performance was thus equivalent whether or not the subjects had previously attempted to guess the patterns (χ^2 (1) = 1.44, p > .10).

These findings imply that the patterns that subjects discovered in their images were largely unexpected, and hence, could be considered "emergent" patterns in the same sense as those described in the previous chapter. In fact, given the more arbitrary nature of the present task, which was designed without regard to particular target patterns or specific mental transformations, it seems even less likely that the reported patterns could be attributed to sophisticated guessing strategies on the part of the subjects.

As an example of the difficulty one might have in predicting these patterns in advance, consider the following set of parts: letter "T", letter "P", and number "8". Without looking at any of the figures, what predictions would you make for

TABLE 3.4
Recognizable and Creative Patterns Reported by Subjects According to Whether They Correctly Predicted Them

Type of Pattern	Predicted	Not Predicted	Total
Recognizable	23	101	124
Creative	4	15	19

Note: The above classifications are based on a total of 280 trials. From Finke and Slayton (1988). From *Memory & Cognition,* Vol. 16, pp. 252–257, reprinted by permission of Psychonomic Society, Inc.

the kinds of patterns that a subject might make out of these parts? I think it extremely unlikely that you could have guessed the creative pattern that a subject actually came up with using these parts, which is shown in Fig. 3.4, along with other examples of creative patterns in this experiment. (In fact, over the past 3 years, I have asked hundreds of students and colleagues to try to predict this and other examples of the more striking creative patterns, and no one has yet been able to do so.)

Table 3.5 lists the many different kinds of patterns that subjects reported in these experiments (112 in all), along with their relative frequencies. There were a grand total of 53 creative patterns; 69.8% of these occurred with a frequency of 2 or less, whereas this was true for only 20% of those patterns that were correctly predicted by the subjects or the experimenter. Thus, the creative patterns tended to be relatively uncommon, whereas the patterns that were predicted were likely to be those that were frequently reported.

Another feature of these experiments is that success on the task did not improve with practice, reflecting the apparent spontaneity with which the image discoveries were made. The number of recognizable patterns reported did not

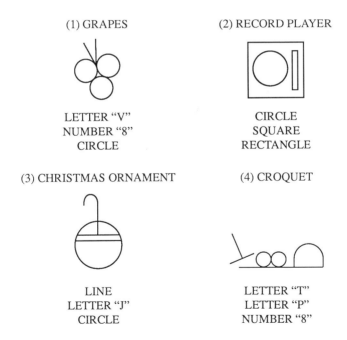

(1) GRAPES

LETTER "V"
NUMBER "8"
CIRCLE

(2) RECORD PLAYER

CIRCLE
SQUARE
RECTANGLE

(3) CHRISTMAS ORNAMENT

LINE
LETTER "J"
CIRCLE

(4) CROQUET

LETTER "T"
LETTER "P"
NUMBER "8"

FIG. 3.4. Examples of creative patterns that subjects discovered but were not able to predict, together with the sets of parts that were used in the mental synthesis. (From Finke & Slayton, 1988, *Memory & Cognition*, Vol. 16, pp. 252–257, reprinted by permission of Psychonomic Society, Inc.)

TABLE 3.5
Frequency of Different Types of Recognizable Patterns Reported
in Experiments on Creative Mental Synthesis (Total = 353)

Pattern Name or Category	Frequency	Pattern Name or Category	Frequency
Ice Cream Cone	24	Purse	2
Flag or Pennant	23	Sundae or Soda	2
Letter or Number	22	Table Lamp	2
House	20	Test Tube	2
Table	17	Anchor	1
TV Set	15	Baseball	1
Umbrella	15	Bell	1
Face	11	Belt Buckle	1
Boat	9	Billboard	1
Tree	9	Birdhouse	1
Cup or Glass	7	Birthday Cake	1
Hat	6	Bowling Ball	1
Lollipop or Popsicle	6	Bulldozer	1
Street Lamp	6	Bullet	1
Antenna	5	Bucket	1
Barbell	5	Bug	1
Door	5	Camera	1
See-Saw	5	Cat	1
Tent or Teepee	5	Chain	1
Bed	4	Christmas Ornament	1
Chair	4	Civil Defense Symbol	1
Traffic Sign	4	Clown	1
Word	4	Coathanger	1
Cart	3	Crib	1
Cross	3	Croquet	1
Gun	3	Domed Stadium	1
Present	3	Earring	1
Snowman	3	Envelope	1
Star	3	Eye Dropper	1
Suitcase	3	Finger	1
Arrow	2	Fish	1
Bomb	2	Fishing Rod	1
Bowtie	2	Grapes	1
Candle	2	Hamburger	1
Coatrack	2	Hammer	1
Diamond	2	Hammock	1
Firecracker	2	Handicapped Parking Symbol	1
Flower	2	Jet	1
Glasses	2	Knife	1
Jack-in-the-Box	2	Loudspeaker	1
Kite	2	Lunch Box	1
Microphone	2	Magnet	1
Mountains	2	Mailbox	1
Mushroom	2	Marshmallow	1
Pie	2	Mickey Mouse	1

Pattern Name or Category	Frequency	Pattern Name or Category	Frequency
Pencil	1	Sine Wave	1
Percentage Sign	1	Skateboard	1
Photographer's Light	1	Skyscraper	1
Pipe	1	Spoon	1
Plunger	1	Syringe	1
Projector Screen	1	Telephone Pole	1
Radio	1	Top	1
Record Player	1	Tripod	1
Satellite Dish	1	Tunnel	1
Sawhorse	1	Watch	1
Shovel	1	Window	1

Note: Data are from Finke and Slayton (1988). From *Memory & Cognition,* Vol. 16, pp. 252–257, reprinted by permission of Psychonomic Society, Inc.

significantly change across the 8 trials, χ^2 (7) = 3.91, $p > .10$, nor did the number of creative patterns, χ^2 (7) = 6.15, $p > .10$. In fact, the absence of practice effects will turn out to be a characteristic of all of the experiments on creative discovery and invention.

COMPARING ACTUAL AND IMAGINED SYNTHESIS

How would the imagined synthesis task compare with that in which people could actually manipulate and combine the parts? In a follow-up study that I conducted in collaboration with Donald Neblett and Harvey Ginsburg, we compared real and imagined synthesis using slight modifications of the Finke and Slayton procedure (Neblett, Finke, & Ginsburg, 1989).

A total of 63 subjects were randomly assigned to one of three conditions: In the Imagined Parts/Mental Synthesis condition, subjects imagined combining the parts while keeping their eyes closed, as in the previous experiments. In the Perceived Parts/Mental Synthesis condition, subjects could look at and manipulate the parts, but could not actually combine them. This was accomplished by printing the parts at one of three sizes on opaque cards that could be positioned and rotated, but not superimposed. In the Perceived Parts/Physical Synthesis condition, subjects could look at, manipulate, and combine the parts. In this case, the parts were printed on transparencies, which could be overlayed to achieve a physical synthesis. In each condition, the subjects could choose any of the three part sizes. There were 8 experimental trials per subject, and the sets of parts were matched across conditions.

The dependent measure, as before, was whether the subjects were able to come up with a recognizable or creative pattern within a 2-minute time period.

It was decided not to use the actual time required for completing the synthesis as the dependent measure, or the number of patterns that one could generate in a given period, because in the perceptual conditions this would depend to some degree on the subjects' dexterity in handling the cards and overlays. Rather, it was assumed that 2 minutes would provide a reasonable amount of time for subjects to come up with at least one recognizable pattern in each condition.

Table 3.6 presents the results of the study. Recognizable patterns were reported on 44% of the trials, similar to the proportion obtained by Finke and Slayton (1988), who had used the same criteria but a different set of judges. Of these, 18, or 8.1%, were classified as creative patterns. Performance in the Imagined Parts/Mental Synthesis and Perceived Parts/Physical Synthesis conditions was statistically equivalent (χ^2 (1) < 1). Significantly fewer patterns were reported in the Perceived Parts/Mental Synthesis condition (χ^2 (2) = 6.81, p < .05), where the parts could be physically manipulated but had to be mentally combined. As before, there were no practice effects across the experimental trials in any of the conditions (p > .05 for all χ^2 tests for the effects of trial order).

As in Finke and Slayton (1988), post-experimental questionnaires indicated that the predominant strategy was to combine the parts by trial and error until a resulting pattern could be recognized (reported by 74.5% of the subjects), as opposed to first thinking of a possible pattern suggested by the parts, and then trying to assemble the parts to make that pattern. Again, the nature of the task itself apparently stimulates one to search for interesting part combinations that can eventually lead to emergent patterns. Examples of creative patterns that were reported in this study are shown in Fig. 3.5.

The findings of the Neblett, Finke, and Ginsburg (1989) study suggest that in these types of tasks, mental synthesis is at least as effective as an actual physical synthesis. In other words, there seems to be no particular advantage to physically combining the parts, compared to simply imagining the combinations, when attempting to discover recognizable or creative patterns. Strictly speaking, however, this conclusion would apply only to cases where small numbers of parts are imagined. The reason, as discussed in the previous chapter, is that there are limits on the number of parts a person can maintain in an image at any one time.

TABLE 3.6

Recognizable and Creative Patterns Reported by Subjects According to Whether They Perceived or Imagined the Parts and Whether the Synthesis was Mental or Physical

Type of Pattern	Imagined Parts Mental Synthesis	Perceived Parts Mental Synthesis	Perceived Parts Physical Synthesis
Recognizable	80	56	86
Creative	8	4	6

Note: The above classifications are based on a total of 504 trials, 168 per condition. From Neblett, Finke, and Ginsburg (1989).

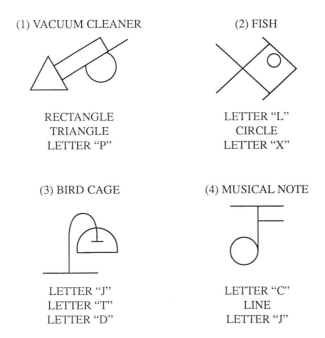

(1) VACUUM CLEANER

RECTANGLE
TRIANGLE
LETTER "P"

(2) FISH

LETTER "L"
CIRCLE
LETTER "X"

(3) BIRD CAGE

LETTER "J"
LETTER "T"
LETTER "D"

(4) MUSICAL NOTE

LETTER "C"
LINE
LETTER "J"

FIG. 3.5. Examples of creative patterns that subjects discovered in experiments on comparing mental and physical synthesis, together with the sets of parts that were used in the mental synthesis. (From Neblett, Finke, & Ginsburg, 1989.)

These findings are in general agreement with those referred to earlier showing that imagery and perception can often be considered functionally equivalent processes (e.g., Finke, 1980; Shepard, 1984). But what about the poorer performance of subjects in the Perceived Parts/Mental Synthesis condition? This is in the spirit of other findings that have demonstrated that perceptual processes can *interfere* with imagery when the imagined and perceived stimuli are mismatched or misaligned (e.g., Brooks, 1968; Finke, 1986b; Segal & Fusella, 1970). In this condition, the parts could be inspected and manipulated, but not actually combined; observing the separated parts could therefore have interfered with the imagined synthesis.

PROVIDING CREATIVE INSPIRATION

Although subjects in these studies were shown several example constructions at the very beginning of the experiments, they were never given examples of possible constructions for the particular sets of parts that were actually used in the experimental trials. One might wonder, therefore, whether giving examples of creative patterns before each trial might inspire the subjects to be more creative when they then attempt to discover recognizable patterns in their own imagined constructions.

Steven Smith and I investigated this question in another follow-up study (Finke & Smith, in preparation), in which we examined the effects of giving example patterns to the subjects, and of varying the kinds of examples. In particular, we were interested in seeing whether giving creative versus noncreative examples had any effect on the subjects' performance.

There were three groups of subjects, with 27 subjects in each group. In the Creative Examples condition, subjects were given the same sets of parts that had led to creative pattern recognitions in the Finke and Slayton (1988) study. After the parts were named, they were shown drawings of the creative patterns as examples of the kinds of patterns one could make out of those parts. They were told, however, that they had to make a pattern different from the one shown in the example. In the Noncreative Examples condition, subjects were also given the same sets of parts, but were shown examples of noncreative patterns that were made out of those parts, again based on judges' ratings in the Finke and Slayton study. Illustrations of both types of example patterns, using the same sets of parts, are given in Fig. 3.6. In the "No Examples" condition, the procedure was identical, except that no examples were provided. Two complete sets of parts were used for the 8 experimental trials; the sets were presented in counterbalanced order, and were matched across conditions. The patterns were scored by three judges in the usual way.

The number of recognizable and creative patterns in each condition are presented in Table 3.7. There were no significant differences among the three conditions, either in terms of the number of recognizable patterns reported, χ^2 (2) = 3.91, $p > .10$, or the number of creative patterns, χ^2 (2) < 1. Also, as before, there were no significant practice effects in any of the conditions ($p > .10$ for all χ^2 tests). Apparently, providing examples of creative patterns before every trial has no appreciable effect on performance, implying that the creative discoveries need not be visually inspired. Examples of some of the creative patterns from this experiment are provided in Fig. 3.7.

There is one aspect of these results that deserves additional comment. The reader may note that, from Table 3.7, the proportion of trials on which recognizable patterns were reported in this experiment, 52.1%, is higher than the proportion for the previous experiments, which ranged from 38.1% to 44.3%. Similarly, the proportion of recognizable patterns that were judged to be creative, 19.8%, is higher than that for the other experiments, which ranged from 8.1% to 16.0%. The reason for these higher percentages is that the sets of parts used in this experiment were taken from trials that had actually led to creative pattern recognitions in the Finke and Slayton study; hence, sets of parts were excluded that might have been, by chance, more difficult to combine into recognizable patterns.

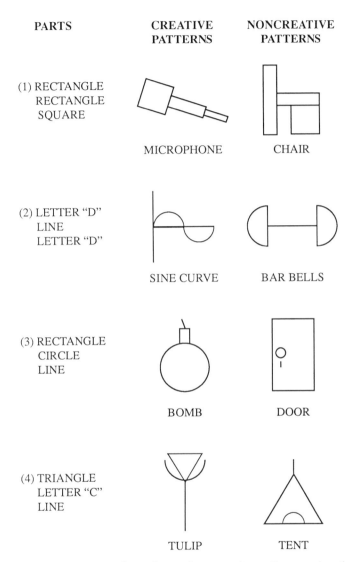

PARTS	CREATIVE PATTERNS	NONCREATIVE PATTERNS
(1) RECTANGLE RECTANGLE SQUARE	MICROPHONE	CHAIR
(2) LETTER "D" LINE LETTER "D"	SINE CURVE	BAR BELLS
(3) RECTANGLE CIRCLE LINE	BOMB	DOOR
(4) TRIANGLE LETTER "C" LINE	TULIP	TENT

FIG. 3.6. Examples of creative and noncreative patterns, using the same sets of parts, that were shown to subjects at the beginning of each trial in experiments on creative inspiration. (From Finke and Smith, in preparation.)

TABLE 3.7
**Recognizable and Creative Patterns According to Whether Subjects
Were Provided With Creative or Noncreative Examples**

Type of Pattern	No Examples	Creative Examples	Noncreative Examples
Recognizable	108	131	105
Creative	23	24	21

Note: The above classifications are based on a total of 648 trials, 216 per condition. From Finke and Smith (in preparation).

SUMMARY

Extending the findings of the previous chapter, these studies show that people are capable of discovering recognizable patterns when exploring the imagined synthesis of randomly chosen parts. Moreover, many of these patterns were strikingly creative—even though the subjects were never told that they should try to be creative, only that the patterns should be recognizable. In addition, the patterns were rarely predicted in advance, either by the experimenter or the

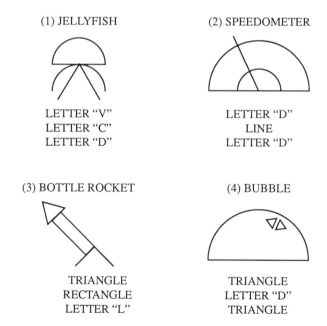

(1) JELLYFISH

LETTER "V"
LETTER "C"
LETTER "D"

(2) SPEEDOMETER

LETTER "D"
LINE
LETTER "D"

(3) BOTTLE ROCKET

TRIANGLE
RECTANGLE
LETTER "L"

(4) BUBBLE

TRIANGLE
LETTER "D"
TRIANGLE

FIG. 3.7. Examples of creative patterns that subjects discovered in experiments on creative inspiration, together with the sets of parts that were used in the mental synthesis. (From Finke and Smith, in preparation).

subjects themselves, they were recognized equally well in imagination as when the parts were physically manipulated and combined, and they were not inspired by having seen other examples of creative patterns. These findings, together with the subjects' reports attesting to the predominant use of trial-and-error exploratory strategies, all reflect the apparent spontaneity of the creative pattern recognitions.

THEORETICAL IMPLICATIONS

One criticism that might be made of these studies is that they really don't *prove* that imagery is being used to make the discoveries, because we did not attempt to isolate the particular mental operations that the subjects employed. In view of the current literature on mental synthesis, however, this would seem to be unnecessary. As discussed at the beginning of this chapter, there is already overwhelming evidence from chronometric studies that pattern recognitions based on the separately presented or described parts of a pattern are achieved by forming a mental image of the assembled pattern. Further, evidence that the eventual pattern recognitions are rarely predictable argues against the possibility that people are merely thinking about associations among the parts in some more abstract way. Indeed, in attempting these tasks for ourselves, my students, my colleagues, and I have repeatedly found that it is virtually impossible to come up with recognizable patterns without first visualizing possible combinations of the parts.

Consistent with the idea that people seldom predict their visual discoveries is the finding that people also have difficulty predicting their eventual successes on problems that require insightful solutions (Metcalfe, 1986). Apparently, part of what it means to arrive at an insightful solution is to be "surprised" at having discovered the solution. And this was often the case for subjects in our experiments; they frequently claimed to have come up with patterns that did not initially occur to them, but which suddenly "emerged" during the exploratory mental synthesis.

In judging the "creativity" of these patterns, a distinction needs to be made between creative combinations of the parts, and creative interpretations of the patterns. For example, the "bowling ball" and "firecracker" patterns shown in Fig. 3.3 represent creative ways of combining the parts, whereas the "bug" and "ice cream soda" patterns are striking because of the way the arrangements of the parts are interpreted. Some patterns, such as the "croquet" pattern shown in Figure 3.4, seem creative in both senses—the parts are creatively arranged, and the pattern is creatively interpreted. Although we did not attempt to separate these aspects of creative discovery in the present experiments on pattern recognition, such an attempt will be made in studies on creative invention considered in the next three chapters.

Creative Inventions in Imagery

The methods developed in the previous studies on creative pattern recognition provide an experimental foundation for exploring the generation of creative inventions in mental imagery. The practical application of these methods will be the main focus throughout the remainder of this book.

In considering the findings on recognizing creative patterns in imagery, I began to wonder whether the same methods could be extended to explore the mental synthesis of novel, practical objects. In particular, could people create entirely new *inventions* simply by imagining interesting combinations of parts, and then "recognizing" useful applications of the resulting imagined forms? If so, the methods could have enormous potential in designing a wide variety of practical objects or devices.

The experimental findings and techniques I describe next will provide readers with a novel approach to creative invention, one that subjects in these experiments have been able to use with considerable success. In fact, upon learning these methods, most people find them to be quite fascinating and continue to use them long after the experiments have been concluded.

A PARADIGM FOR CREATIVE INVENTION
(EXPERIMENTS 1–3)

In the previous experiments, subjects carried out the mental syntheses using flat, two-dimensional forms; although this often led to the discovery of creative objects and patterns, most of these mental creations were of little practical value. Although such findings would no doubt be of interest to artists and creative designers, they would probably not be of much interest, for example, to engineers or inventors. Hence, I decided to modify the previous methods to encourage the invention of three-dimensional objects. Because these procedures are published here for the first time, they will be described in detail.

I began by conducting three experiments, using 60 subjects in each. The subjects were all undergraduate students whose participation fulfilled research requirements in an introductory psychology course. None of the subjects were previously trained in using any of the methods to be described, nor were they selectively recruited.

At the beginning of each experiment, the subjects were given response sheets, which provided spaces for the name of each invention, its drawing, and a description of how the invention works and what its various parts do. They were also given a parts sheet, depicting the 15 parts that would be used in the study. As shown in Fig. 4.1, these consisted of simple three-dimensional forms, such as a "cube," a "half sphere," and a "cone," and various specialized parts, such as a "wire," a "bracket," and a "handle." Each of the parts was described, and the experimenter indicated the specific names that would be used to refer to the parts. For the "wheels" part, it was explained that this always meant a pair of wheels. As in the previous study by Finke and Slayton (1988), there were 1,135 possible unique combinations of the parts. As before, naive experimenters were always used.

There were 6 trials per subject. In most of the experiments, at the beginning of each trial, the experimenter named three of the parts. These were randomly selected by a computer, subject to the following constraints: The parts depicted in the first row of Fig. 4.1, representing the simplest geometric shapes, had a 50% chance of being selected. The parts depicted in the second row, representing the more specialized shapes, had a 33.3% chance of being selected. The parts depicted in the third row, representing the most specialized shapes, had a 16.7% chance of being selected. These decreasing probabilities reduced the chance that all three parts would consist only of the most specialized shapes.

After the experimenter named the three parts, the subjects closed their eyes and were given 2 minutes to mentally assemble the parts to make some kind of useful object, with the emphasis placed on the object's practicality. They had to use all three of the named parts in their mental constructions. If the same part was named twice, or even three times, they had to use that same part the designated number of times. They could vary the size, position, or orientation of any part, but they could not bend or otherwise alter the shape of the parts, with the exception of the "tube" and the "wire," which had been defined as bendable. The parts could vary in their solidity; that is, they could be solid or hollow, opened or closed. They could be attached in any way; one part could even be put inside of another. In addition, the parts could vary in their composition; for example, they could be made of wood, metal, rubber, glass, or any combination of materials.

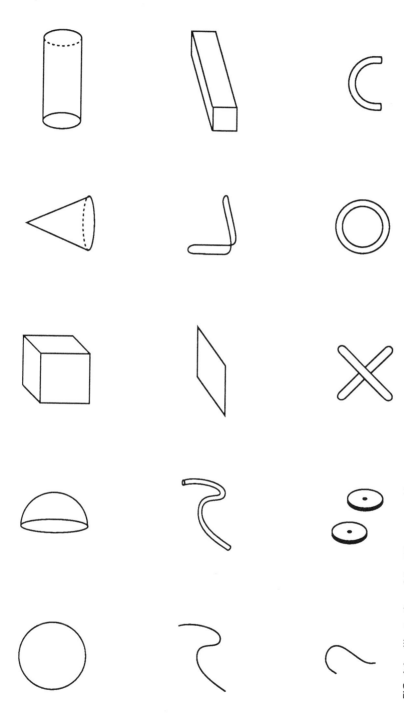

FIG. 4.1. Illustration of the 15 parts used in experiments on creative invention in mental imagery. These were referred to, specifically, by the following names: "SPHERE," "HALF SPHERE," "CUBE," "CONE," "CYLINDER"; "WIRE," "TUBE," "FLAT SQUARE," "BRACKET," "RECTANGULAR BLOCK"; "HOOK," "WHEELS," "CROSS," "RING," and "HANDLE."

The only restriction on the inventions was that the objects had to belong to one of the eight general object categories presented in Table 4.1. Subjects were given a handout listing these allowable categories, with examples provided for each. These categories were chosen to provide for a wide range of possible inventions; they correspond to what have been called "superordinate" object categories in studies on concept formation (e.g., Rosch, Mervis, Gray, Johnson, & Boyes-Braem, 1976).

The subjects were reminded that their task was to come up with a practical invention, if possible, on each trial. At the end of the 2-minute period, the subjects were instructed to open their eyes, and, first, to write down the name of the object on their response sheet. They were then to draw it, and finally to describe the invention, explaining its function and what the parts do. As in the previous studies on creative pattern recognition, the subjects were not allowed to change anything they wrote when naming the object after they had begun to draw it. This procedure was repeated for all 6 trials.

In the first experiment, which will be referred to as the Category Chosen/Parts Random condition, the subjects were restricted in which parts they could use, but could choose whichever category they wanted. In the second experiment, the Category Random/Parts Random condition, the category name was specified along with the parts at the beginning of each trial. That is, the categories were randomly chosen, along with the parts, and the inventions had to belong to the specified category. In the third experiment, the Category Random/Parts Chosen condition, the category was specified at the beginning of each trial, but the subjects were allowed to choose whichever three parts they wanted to use. These three experiments thus spanned the various ways of restricting the parameters of the task.

At no time were the subjects ever told that they should try to be creative in coming up with their inventions. Before the experiment began, they were simply shown four examples of possible inventions; two of these consisted of common objects (e.g., a "drafting pencil" made up of the cone, the rectangular block, and

TABLE 4.1
Allowable Object Categories Used in Experiments
on Creative Inventions

Category	*Examples*
1. FURNITURE	Chairs, Tables, Lamps, etc.
2. PERSONAL ITEMS	Jewelry, Glasses, etc.
3. TRANSPORTATION	Cars, Boats, etc.
4. SCIENTIFIC INSTRUMENTS	Measuring Devices, etc.
5. APPLIANCES	Washing Machines, Toasters, etc.
6. TOOLS AND UTENSILS	Screwdrivers, Spoons, etc.
7. WEAPONS	Guns, Missles, etc.
8. TOYS AND GAMES	Baseball Bats, Dolls, etc.

the cylinder), and two consisted of novel objects (e.g., a "back massager" made up of the wheels, the rectangular block, and the sphere.) It was emphasized only that the invention had to be a practical object or device.

JUDGING THE INVENTIONS

Because of the very large number of inventions that would have to be rated in this and later studies (over 2,500 for all of the experiments on creative invention), only two judges were used this time, rather than three. These judges were both experienced in rating creative patterns from the previous experiments, and they spent nearly a month independently studying and rating the inventions. Though tedious, this task was not without its rewards, in that many of the inventions turned out to be quite remarkable. The judges commented, in fact, that it was like going on a "treasure hunt" for new inventions; this made the rating task much more tolerable.

The inventions were rated along two dimensions, using a 5-point scale: *Practicality*, which referred to how practical the invention was, and *Originality*, which referred to how original the invention was. The exact rating scales are given in Table 4.2. The two types of ratings were to be regarded as distinct. That is, an object could be very practical and not original, or not practical but very original; similarly, an object could be very practical and also very original, or neither practical nor original. Additional instructions stressed judging the way the parts of the object were put together and how they functioned, rather than how well the object was drawn, and judging the overall design of the object, rather than whether the object had all of the working parts it would actually need. Finally, if an object was constructed using the wrong parts, or only some of the parts, or was drawn and not described, it was not to be rated.

All inventions reported in these and later experiments were rated together in random order, without knowledge of the experimental conditions. This was done so that meaningful comparisons could be made across the different experiments. The inventions were classified in the following way: If an invention received a

TABLE 4.2
Rating Scales Used by Judges for Assessing the Practicality
and Originality of the Subjects' Inventions

PRACTICALITY:	ORIGINALITY:
5 Very Practical	5 Very Original
4 Practical	4 Original
3 Somewhat Practical	3 Somewhat Original
2 Marginally Practical	2 Marginally Original
1 Not Practical at All	1 Not Original at All

total rating score of at least "9" between the two judges on the Practicality dimension, it was classified as a "Practical Invention." If a practical invention also received a total rating score of at least "8" between the judges on the Originality dimension, it was further classified as a "Creative Invention." If a creative invention received the very highest ratings from both judges on both dimensions (a total score of 10 for each rating), it was classified as a "Highly Creative Invention." This provided for a conservative rating system, placing greater emphasis on the practicality of the inventions. For example, it excluded inventions which one judge considered practical whereas the other did not. Also, it meant that both judges had to agree that a practical invention was also original before it could be classified as "creative."

Of course, requiring agreement among judges that certain inventions are creative does not guarantee that they would be universally regarded as such. That is why I shall provide numerous examples of objects that were classified as creative inventions—particularly, those rated as "highly creative"— so that readers may decide for themselves. In any event, the more important consideration is that the same criteria for judging the patterns was applied across the different experimental conditions. This permits one to evaluate, comparatively, the consequences of changing various restrictions on the task.

INTUITIVE PREDICTIONS

Given the three experimental conditions described earlier in this chapter, which one would you expect to yield the greatest number of creative inventions? In designing this study, my own prediction was that any constraints that were imposed on the mental constructions would enhance the creative potential of the task. Thus, for example, subjects should be more creative when the parts are specified randomly than when they are free to select them for themselves. This prediction makes intuitive sense; having to work with an arbitrary set of parts would force one to consider novel combinations of the parts—as suggested by the previous studies on creative pattern recognition. Similarly, restricting the object category would further discourage conventional ways of thinking about possible inventions that could be made using a particular set of parts. For some, however, this might seem counterintuitive, in that restricting both the parts and the object category might severely limit the kinds of inventions that subjects were capable of discovering. Yet, this technique worked surprisingly well.

COMPARING RESULTS AMONG THE EXPERIMENTS

Table 4.3 presents the number of practical inventions, creative inventions, and highly creative inventions generated in the three experiments. First, there were no significant differences among the experimental conditions in the number of practical inventions ($\chi^2 (2) = 1.04$, ns). However, as Table 4.3 shows, there were significant differences among the experiments in both the number of creative inventions ($\chi^2 (2) = 15.92, p < .01$), and the number of highly creative inventions

TABLE 4.3
Number of Practical, Creative, and Highly Creative Inventions
Reported by Subjects According to Whether the Parts and Object
Categories were Chosen or Randomly Specified (Experiments 1–3)

Type of Invention	Condition		
	Category Chosen *Parts Random*	*Category Random* *Parts Random*	*Category Random* *Parts Chosen*
Practical	191	175	193
Creative	31	49	17
Highly Creative	11	14	3

Note: The above categorizations are based on a total of 1,080 trials, 360 for each condition. "Creative" inventions were practical inventions that were rated as original; "Highly Creative" inventions received the highest possible rating on both practicality and originality.

$(\chi^2 (2) = 6.93, p < .05)$. The greatest number of creative inventions (49) and highly creative inventions (14) were obtained when both the parts and the object categories were restricted. In contrast, the fewest number of creative inventions (17) and highly creative inventions (3) occurred when the subjects were free to choose their own parts.

The lack of significant differences among the experimental conditions in the number of practical inventions suggests that the task itself was not necessarily harder when the parts and the object categories were restricted, compared to when the parts could be chosen. Rather, these restrictions simply resulted in a higher proportion of *creative* inventions relative to the practical inventions (28% vs. 8.8%). Evidently, such restrictions served to improve the creative quality of the inventions.

In Experiment 2, the Category Random/Parts Random condition, the subjects were able to come up with a creative invention on 13.6% of the trials. This is all the more remarkable given the extraordinary nature of the task: naive, untrained subjects given only 2 minutes per trial to discover an invention, and without being able to choose either the parts or the object category.

Finally, as in the previous experiments, there was no evidence at all for any learning or practice effects across any of the experimental trials (for all χ^2 tests, $p > .10$). This again reflects the spontaneity of the discoveries and the use of "trial-and-error" combinational strategies.

EXAMPLES OF CREATIVE INVENTIONS

I next present specific examples of some of the inventions that were classified as "highly creative." First, Table 4.4 lists the names of all of the creative inventions for the three experiments. They represent a striking variety of novel, interesting objects and devices, most exhibiting simple, elegant concepts in design. Of the

TABLE 4.4
List of Inventions Classified as Creative and Highly Creative
(Experiments 1–3)

* baseball target
  bouncing chair (2)
* bread kneader
* butter utensil
  campfire pot (2)
* cat enticer
  cat palace
* CHILDPROOF BOWL
  children's gerbil cage
* clothespin holder
  coiled spring chair
  conical car
* conical egg beater
  conical rattle
* decorative fishtank
  dexterity trainer
  dough roller
  drying rack
  dual spinning top
* dual toothpick
  earthquake detector
  elevated condiment tray
  elevated wash basin
  exotic earring (2)
  exploding num-chucks
  fighting pick
  fingernail cleaner
  food warmer
  funnel slide
* grip grinder
* HAMBURGER MAKER
  hammer hook
* hammer spreader
  hand edger
  hand mixer
  hand weapon
* HANDICAPPED EXERCISER
* HANGING EXTENSION CORD
  hanging plant holder
  hanging seat
  headrest couch
* HIP EXERCISER
  hook funnel
* hook ball
  hooked club
  illuminated keychain
* inhalation tester
  knotted hairclip

* LAND SLED
  magnetic flux measurer
  magnetic pitcher
  measuring roller
  meat pounder
  mini-skewer
* modern cradle
* moving basketball goal
* mutual rocking chair
  neon desk lamp
* pie crust cutter
  pivoting table
  plant waterer
* PORTABLE PLAY POOL
  portable towel holder
  portable steamer
  pressure intake valve
  pressurized trash compactor
  rain funnel
  rain gauge
  retractable sword
  ring mixer
  ring wagon
  roller tenderizer
* SHOESTRING UNLACER
  SLIDE COORDINATOR
  solar shower
  spectrum displayer
  spherical bassinet
  spherical doll
  spherical traffic sign
* SPHERICAL TRAVEL CAGE
* spinning snow sled
  splashproof pot
  sponge toothbrush
  stabilized funnel
* stereo chair
  suspendable crib
  table couch
  toothbrush holder
  toothpaste dispenser
  tube chair
  tube juicer
  wall-mounted work bench
  watch displayer
* water dispenser
  weeble wobble tree

Note: Creative inventions that were also classified as "Highly Creative" are denoted by an asterisk. The creative inventions that are described in the text are capitalized.

97 creative inventions, all but three were unique. The majority of these inventions corresponded to clever, practical objects that one could find useful in everyday life situations.

Figure 4.2, for example, shows the design that one subject came up with for a "childproof bowl." The large, flat base of the bowl makes it relatively spillproof; the hook allows the bowl to be secured to the top of a table or a high chair, or to be hung from a wall or cabinet for storage. It is a simple design, yet extremely practical. I can easily imagine mothers of young children wishing they had one.

Figure 4.3 presents a clever design for a "hamburger maker." One half of the utensil, the open half sphere, is used to scoop out a measured amount of hamburger meat; the other half, the solid sphere, is used to roll and press the meat into a pattie. The utensil would have obvious uses in fast-food restaurants.

In Fig. 4.4 there is a design for a "handicapped exerciser," consisting of a metal ring, a rubber ball, and an elastic tube. This exerciser can be used in a variety of ways by the physically impaired. For example, the ring can be placed over a doorknob or wheelchair arm and the ball can be pulled to improve arm strength, or one can place one's foot inside the ring, while holding onto the ball, and bend the knees to exercise the legs. Also, the ball can be squeezed to improve one's grip.

Figure 4.5 presents the "hanging extension cord," a very practical idea for the home or workshop. This allows an extension cord to be easily accessible, while keeping it out of the way when not in use.

Figure 4.6 presents one of my favorite inventions, the "hip exerciser." You use this device by standing on the half sphere, holding onto the rectangular post, and shifting your weight from side to side. The wire connects the top of the device to the walls to keep it from falling over.

A "land sled" is presented in Fig. 4.7. This serves as a sled for those who live in places where there is no snow. Although the design may need some further refinement, the basic idea is very clever.

The "portable play pool" is shown in Fig. 4.8. Children sit inside the hollow half-sphere, while the cone draws water from below and sprays it back into the pool. The cone also provides support for climbing in and out of the pool, and the wheels make it portable. The water level can be kept shallow for safe use with very young children.

A practical invention for parents and children is the "shoestring unlacer," shown in Fig. 4.9. This simple utensil can be carried in a pocket; it can also serve as a key chain. The hooked end makes it easy to untie a knotted shoelace.

A final example of a "highly creative" invention is the "spherical travel cage," shown in Fig. 4.10. The spherical interior can rotate, so that a pet will suffer minimum discomfort from rocking motions while traveling in a plane or boat.

There is another invention I would like to describe, which, although not classified as "highly" creative, is nevertheless quite interesting. This is the "slide coordinator," shown in Fig. 4.11. Children jump off the platform and try to grab

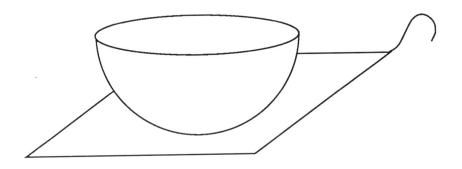

FIG. 4.2.   The "childproof bowl," constructed using the HALF SPHERE, FLAT SQUARE, and HOOK. The large, flat base of the bowl prevents a child from accidentally spilling the contents, and the hook can be used to secure the bowl to a table or a high chair.

FIG. 4.3. A "hamburger maker," constructed using the SPHERE, HALF SPHERE, and CYLINDER. The opposite ends of the utensil are used to measure the hamburger meat and to roll it into a pattie.

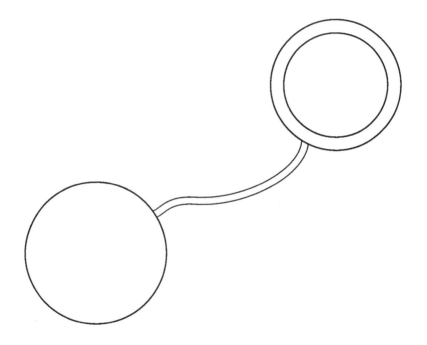

FIG. 4.4. A "handicapped exerciser," constructed using the SPHERE, TUBE, and RING. By pulling on the rubber ball while the ring is attached to a stationary object or the foot, a handicapped person can begin physical therapy.

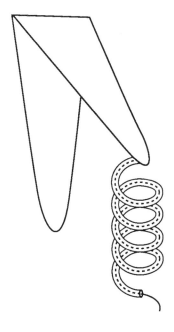

FIG. 4.5. The "hanging extension cord," constructed using the WIRE, TUBE, and BRACKET. This allows easy access to an extension cord while keeping the cord out of the way when not needed.

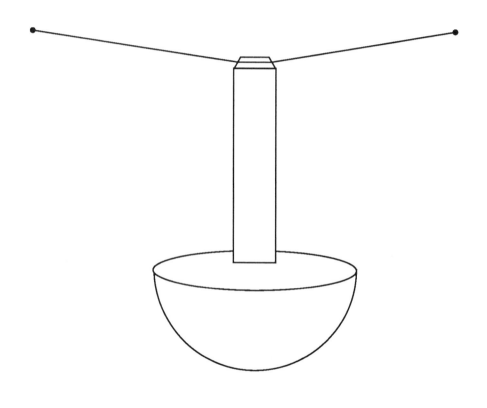

FIG. 4.6. The "hip exerciser," constructed using the HALF SPHERE, WIRE, and RECT-ANGULAR BLOCK. By shifting one's weight from side to side while standing on the device, one can exercise one's hips.

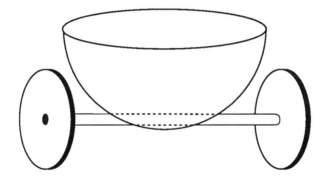

FIG. 4.7.   A "land sled," constructed using the HALF SPHERE, TUBE, and WHEELS. Can be used in place of an actual sled for those who live in areas without snow.

FIG. 4.8. The "portable play pool," constructed using the HALF SPHERE, CONE, and WHEELS. Water is sprayed up from the cone, and the wheels make it portable.

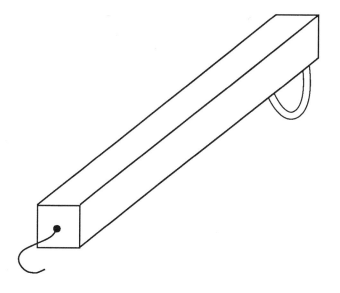

FIG. 4.9. The "shoestring unlacer," constructed using the RECTANGULAR BLOCK, HOOK, and HANDLE. Parents and children can use this simple utensil to untie a knotted shoe lace.

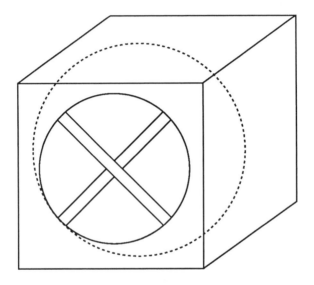

FIG. 4.10. The "spherical travel cage," constructed using the SPHERE, CUBE, and CROSS. Pets can be transported with minimal discomfort resulting from rocking motions, as the spherical interior can rotate to compensate.

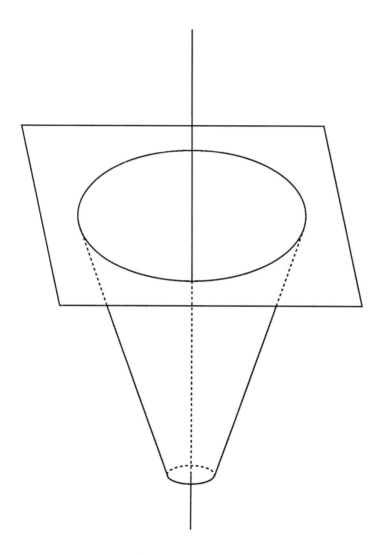

FIG. 4.11. The "slide coordinator," constructed using the FLAT SQUARE, CONE, and WIRE. Children try to grab the "rope" as they jump off the platform; if they miss, they simply slide down the conical slide.

hold of the rope. If they miss, they slide down the conical slide and land on a soft surface below. The idea is that the children can learn to improve their coordination while having fun.

ASPECTS OF INDIVIDUAL PERFORMANCE

In the most successful experiment (Experiment 2), where both the parts and categories were specified randomly, 40% of the subjects were able to come up with at least one creative invention. The techniques can therefore be applied quite generally. Some of the subjects, moreover, seemed particularly talented at the task. In that experiment, for example, out of a total of 60 subjects, 5 came up with at least three creative inventions out of the six trials, and 13 came up with at least two.

The reports that subjects gave in these experiments were similar to those in the previous studies on creative pattern recognitions. In those conditions where the parts were specified randomly, the subjects claimed that the most successful strategy was to imagine interesting shapes and forms made up of the three parts, and then to try to interpret the forms as particular kinds of inventions, in contrast to starting out with a specific invention in mind and then trying to make the parts conform to it. The idea of combining the parts before knowing what the invention will be leads to the most important discovery in all of the creative invention experiments; this will be considered later in Chapter 6.

READER PARTICIPATION: CREATIVE INVENTIONS

I would now like to give readers the opportunity to try the task for themselves, to attempt to come up with their own inventions. Table 4.5 lists sets of parts that might appear on a typical trial in these experiments. The parts shown in this table have not been screened or preselected in any way; hence they recreate the kinds of trial sequences that would have actually existed in the experiments.

To simulate the procedure of the first experiment, that in which the parts were specified but the category could be chosen, close your eyes after reading the names of the parts, and allow yourself 2 minutes to come up with some kind of practical object or device belonging to any of the eight categories listed in Table 4.1. Remember that the parts can be combined in any way, can be of any size, and may consist of any material. Then write down the name of the invention, draw it, and describe it. A total of 10 example trials are provided.

To simulate the conditions of the second experiment, where both the parts and the category were specified randomly, use the parts listed in Table 4.6, which include a category name. This time, the invention or device must belong to the category that is specified along with the parts.

TABLE 4.5
Examples of Sets of Parts Used in Experiments on Creative
Invention in Which the Parts Were Randomly Specified but the
Category Could be Chosen

1.	SPHERE CONE CONE		6.	RECTANGULAR BLOCK CUBE RECTANGULAR BLOCK
2.	SPHERE FLAT SQUARE HANDLE		7.	WHEELS HALF SPHERE SPHERE
3.	HALF SPHERE RING RECTANGULAR BLOCK		8.	WIRE HALF SPHERE CUBE
4.	BRACKET HALF SPHERE RECTANGULAR BLOCK		9.	HOOK HANDLE CONE
5.	HANDLE WIRE CUBE		10	SPHERE FLAT SQUARE CYLINDER

SUMMARY

The experiments reported in this chapter demonstrate that these simple imagery techniques can actually lead one to discover creative inventions. The most successful technique is that in which both the parts and object category are randomly specified, which places the greatest restrictions on the task. Evidently, restricting the allowable parts and categories demands that one consider design possibilities that are less conventional—and hence, that are likely to be more creative.

One thing that subjects often commented on was that the inventions they reported were not necessarily in their final form, but rather, represented the essential concept or idea underlying the invention. Many of them, in fact, expressed a desire to work on their designs further, under less restrictive conditions. Some of them even reported that it was difficult *not* to think about their designs, like a melody that stays in one's mind. It appears that these techniques not only inspire ideas for new inventions; they also create interest and motivation in pursuing the ideas to fulfillment.

THEORETICAL IMPLICATIONS

The cleverness and originality of most of these inventions, together with the previous control procedures, suggests that the inventions cannot be attributed to simple guessing or to purely conceptual associations among the parts. Rather, successful performance evidently depends on forming a mental image, "inspect-

TABLE 4.6
Examples of Sets of Parts Used in Experiments
on Creative Invention in Which Both the Parts and the Category
Were Randomly Specified

1.	HANDLE FLAT SQUARE HALF SPHERE TOOLS AND UTENSILS	6.	HANDLE CONE TUBE TOOLS AND UTENSILS	
2.	WIRE TUBE WHEELS WEAPONS	7	HALF SPHERE CROSS CYLINDER FURNITURE	
3.	HOOK CYLINDER SPHERE SCIENTIFIC INSTRUMENTS	8.	HOOK HALF SPHERE RECTANGULAR BLOCK TOYS AND GAMES	
4.	RING SPHERE TUBE FURNITURE	9.	CYLINDER CYLINDER FLAT SQUARE APPLIANCES	
5.	CONE SPHERE CYLINDER APPLIANCES	10.	SPHERE CYLINDER TUBE TRANSPORTATION	

ing" the image, and "recognizing" its emergent properties. Again, to verify this, readers are invited to attempt the task while trying not to use imagery, or to try to guess any of the creative inventions from the sets of parts used in their construction.

There is nothing special about the particular parts that were used in these experiments, except that they could be easily named and were already familiar to the subjects. I would expect, therefore, that other kinds of parts could be used with equal success under the right conditions. For example, the "generalized cones" proposed by Marr and Nishihara (1978), or the "geons" proposed by Biederman (1987) might work equally well, given that people would have sufficient familiarity with them.

The way subjects would often suddenly realize what their imagined forms could be used for is reminiscent of so-called "aha" experiences during problem solving (e.g., Gardner, 1978; Metcalfe, 1986). These kinds of sudden insights typically occur in tasks that are designed to break up conventional ways of thinking, as in studies on "Einstellung" or "functional fixedness" (e.g., Adams, 1974; Hayes, 1981; Levine, 1987). However, the techniques developed here are distinct from those normally used in problem-solving studies, where solutions to a specific problem are sought. In contrast, the present task does not define what constitutes a correct solution; it only places restrictions on the general kinds of inventions and the parts that can be used. In other words, these inventions are not task-specific; rather, they represent natural responses to a creative opportunity. The resulting inventions can lead one later on to consider the kinds of problems that the inventions might solve. This idea is taken up again in the final chapter.

Chapter
5

Restricted Imagery Inventions

Two main ideas were presented in the previous chapter. The first is that restricting the choices a person has, concerning what parts and object categories to use, leads to inventions that are more creative. To return to an earlier analogy, consider a person on some deserted island who has only a restrictive set of raw materials to work with, and who must consider general needs like shelter, tools, weapons, and transportation. Such conditions would tend to inspire inventions that are creative and resourceful, compared to those that might be conceived when materials are abundant and the needs not so urgent.

Second, there is the idea that the best strategy for coming up with creative inventions is not to think about a specific kind of invention initially, but to consider interesting combinations of parts and then seeing whether the resulting objects can be interpreted as something useful within a general category. This reflects the notion of "combinational play" in creative thinking. The implication is that it is better not to have a particular object in mind when you start out trying to invent something.

These ideas lead in two directions, to be considered separately in this and the following chapter. For the moment, consider what would happen if you further restricted the kinds of objects that one could invent. You could do this in one of two ways. First, you could specify the particular *type* of object within a general category; for example, specifying that the object must be a "chair," rather than "furniture." Or, you could specify, within a category, the particular *function* of the object; for example, that the object must be a "piece of furniture that a handicapped person could use." The present chapter examines and compares the effects of restricting the inventions in these two ways.

RESTRICTING OBJECT TYPES (EXPERIMENT 4)

Eleanor Rosch and her students have identified a class of objects, called "basic objects," which are subsets of the larger, superordinate object categories, and which have the following characteristics: Members of basic object categories possess many of the same features in common, they are manipulated in similar ways, they have similar shapes, and they can be identified by the average shape of the other members of the category (Rosch et al., 1976). In addition, basic objects are the most inclusive members of a category for which mental images of the category as a whole can be formed. Examples of basic objects would be things like a "table," a "car," and a "hammer," within the superordinate categories "furniture," "vehicles," and "tools." Experiment 4 was designed to see whether restricting the categories to basic object types would affect how successfully people could use the previous methods to discover creative inventions.

The experimental procedure consisted of a simple variation of that for Experiment 2, the Parts Random/Category Random condition of the previous chapter. Recall that in that experiment both the parts and object categories were randomly specified at the beginning of each trial. In the present experiment, this procedure was repeated, except that now the types of objects were specified, rather than the general object categories. Table 5.1 presents the various object types that were

TABLE 5.1
Object Types Specified for Each Object Category (Experiment 4)

FURNITURE	APPLIANCES
Chair	Dishwasher
Table	Food Processor
Lamp	Washing Machine
Clock	Vacuum Cleaner
Bed	Toaster
PERSONAL ITEMS	TOOLS AND UTENSILS
Jewelry	Hammer
Wallet	Spoon
Pencil	Can Opener
Camera	Shovel
TRANSPORTATION	WEAPONS
Car	Gun
Boat	Bomb
Aircraft	Missile
Bicycle	Knife
Sled	Shield
SCIENTIFIC INSTRUMENTS	TOYS AND GAMES
Rain Gauge	Doll
Thermometer	Frisbee
Telescope	Dart Game
Sound Amplifier	Baby Toy

used. Sixty subjects were run using six trials per subject, and the inventions were rated as in the previous experiments.

RESTRICTING OBJECT FUNCTIONS (EXPERIMENT 5)

In Experiment 5, this same procedure was repeated with a new group of 60 subjects, except that this time the functions of the objects were specified, rather then the types of objects. This was done by matching each object type in Experiment 4 with an object function in Experiment 5, so that the general object categories would be equally represented across the experimental trials. The functions were always defined using the format of first identifying the general object category and then specifying what the object does or how it works; for example, "A weapon that uses light." The various object functions that were included in the experiment are presented in Table 5.2.

What predictions might one make for the relative success of these two experiments? Because members of basic object categories share more features in common than members of superordinate categories (e.g., Rosch et al., 1976), the features of basic objects are more restricted. Because the object parts in these experiments are selected at random, the task should therefore be more difficult when the object types are specified, since the parts may not conform at all to the defining features of the object. This would be less of a problem, however, if only the function of the object were specified within a general category. Thus, my prediction was that subjects ought to do worse when the object types were restricted than when only the object categories or the object functions were restricted.

RESULTS OF THE EXPERIMENTS

Table 5.3 presents the results of these two experiments. First, a greater number of practical inventions were obtained when the object functions had been specified than when the object types had been specified, $\chi^2 (1) = 4.65, p < .05$. However, both of these conditions yielded fewer practical inventions than Experiment 2, where just the object categories had been restricted, $\chi^2 (1) = 17.50$ and 39.05, respectively; $p < .001$. Compared with Experiment 2, where subjects had come up with a practical invention on 48.6% of the trials, subjects were able to come up with a practical invention on only 29.2% of the trials in Experiment 5, and on only 21.1% of the trials in Experiment 4. Thus, there appear to be limits on how far one can restrict the conditions of the task.

In considering the number of creative inventions that resulted, a slightly different pattern emerges. First, as with the practical inventions, subjects came up with significantly more creative inventions when functions were specified (51)

TABLE 5.2
Object Functions Specified for Each Object Category (Experiment 5)

FURNITURE

A piece of furniture that a pet could use.
A piece of furniture that could also play music.
A piece of furniture that a handicapped person could use.
A piece of furniture that would help you wake up.
A piece of furniture that you could enjoy looking at.

PERSONAL ITEMS

A personal item you could wear at the beach.
A personal item you could use to record your thoughts.
A personal item that would have sentimental value.
A personal item that you could use to solve problems.

TRANSPORTATION

A vehicle for travelling up a mountain.
A vehicle that could be used in very bad weather.
A vehicle that could travel over very rough terrain.
A vehicle you could power by yourself.
A vehicle for lifting another person.

SCIENTIFIC INSTRUMENTS

A device that tells you when the weather changes.
A device that magnifies things.
A device that detects earthquakes.
A device that amplifies sound.

APPLIANCES

An appliance that would help you cook dinner.
An appliance that could catch a burglar.
An appliance that would clean your furniture.
An appliance that would heat your home.
An appliance you could use for taking a shower.

TOOLS AND UTENSILS

A tool that a schoolteacher might use.
A utensil for making a sandwich.
A tool for removing snow.
A utensil for mixing ingredients.

WEAPONS

A weapon that uses light.
A weapon you could hide in your pocket.
A weapon that doesn't make any noise.
A weapon you could use underwater.
A weapon you would only use in self defense.

TOYS AND GAMES

A toy two babies could play with.
A game you could play with a ball.
A toy for a large dog.
A game that a blind person would enjoy.

TABLE 5.3
Number of Practical, Creative, and Highly Creative Inventions
Reported by Subjects According to Whether Object Types
or Object Functions Were Specified (Experiments 4–5)

Type of Invention	Condition	
	Object Type Specified	Object Function Specified
Practical	76	105
Creative	20	51
Highly Creative	1	11

Note: The above categorizations are based on a total of 720 trials, 360 for each condition. "Creative" inventions were practical inventions rated as original; "Highly Creative" inventions received the highest possible rating on both practicality and originality.

than when types were specified (20), $\chi^2 = 13.54$, $p < .001$. Of the 12 highly creative inventions that were reported, all but one came from Experiment 5, where the object functions had been specified. In addition, there were significantly fewer creative inventions when object types had been specified than in Experiment 2, where only the object categories had been, $\chi^2 (1) = 12.19, p < .05$. However, the number of creative inventions when the functions had been specified within the categories was statistically equivalent to that when just the categories had been specified ($\chi^2 (1) < 1$; compare Tables 4.3 and 5.3). Thus, whereas restricting the object functions reduced the overall number of practical inventions, it did not reduce the number of creative inventions.

With regard to individual performance, nearly one-third of the subjects in Experiment 4 (31.7%) were able to come up with at least one creative invention, whereas 50% of the subjects in Experiment 5 had been able to do so. In the latter experiment, 21.7% of the subjects came up with two or more creative inventions. As before, there were no practice effects in either experiment (for all χ^2 tests for the effects of trial order, $p > .10$).

EXAMPLES OF CREATIVE INVENTIONS

Table 5.4 presents a list of all the creative inventions generated in these two experiments. Of the 71 inventions, 58 were unique. Duplications of creative inventions were restricted to just four of the experimental trials, where, by chance, the particular sets of parts, together with the way the objects were specified, had suggested the same kind of invention to more than one subject. However, all of the inventions that had been rated as "highly creative" were unique. Examples of these are the following:

TABLE 5.4
List of Inventions Classified as Creative and Highly Creative
(Experiments 4–5)

* airflow fireplace	magnetic wallet
baby pull-up bar	magnifying goggles
bean-bag recliner	meat slicer
bicycle wind breaker	memory rain gauge
BLADED FLASHLIGHT	movement sensor
blind ball boomer	notebook lamp
blow-gun darts	* OMNIDIRECTIONAL COUCH
bookend lamp	portable vacuum
cat swatter	ring chair
chamber bomb	roaming mine
child peeker	* sandwich mate
circular bread cutter	* security wallet
circular stove	SEISMIC SPHERE
conical picture frame	self-emptying bed pan
continuous food processor	* SNOW VACUUM
* CRUST REMOVER	SOLAR HEATER
cup catcher	* space saver dispenser
cushioned sled	* STOVE FIRE EXTINGUISHER
distance measurer	straw bowl
* DOORKNOB ALARM	suction climber
dual dipper	toy jet
fletching darts	tug-of-war (6)
food retriever	turbo sled
frisbee top	universal dispenser
* GUTTER CLEANER	water frisbee
hand shovel	weather catcher (2)
hand snow plow	weather dish
handle ball (3)	weighted frisbee (2)
hot liquid pourer	windchime chair
* IMAGINARY PET	wobble doll
jewelry pedistal	

Note: Creative inventions that were also classified as "Highly Creative" are denoted by an asterisk. The creative inventions that are described in the text are capitalized.

Figure 5.1 presents a "crust remover." The solid cube is placed over pieces of bread, making it easy to remove the crust, while the other half of the utensil contains two rotating blades for removing the plastic wrapping around meats, such as bologna, or the moldy edges around cheeses.

Figure 5.2 presents an invention that I regard as one of the more clever in this series. This is a "doorknob alarm" that consists of a doorknob cover containing heat or motion sensors. This device would be extremely effective in deterring a burglar, since there is no point in breaking a lock if you can't touch the doorknob. Also, the device could be easily removed and placed on other doors as needed.

FIG. 5.1. A "crust remover," constructed using the CUBE, WHEELS, and CONE, under the restriction that it had to be "a utensil for making a sandwich." The cube is placed on slices of bread to remove the crust, and the cutting wheels are used to remove the outer edges from slices of meat and cheese.

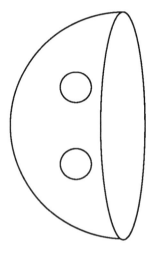

FIG. 5.2. A "doorknob alarm," constructed using the SPHERE, SPHERE, and HALF SPHERE, under the restriction that it had to be "an appliance that would catch a burgler." The half sphere is a cover that is placed over a doorknob, and the small spheres that are attached to the cover are heat or motion sensitive.

In Fig. 5.3 there is a design for a "gutter cleaner," a simple tool with a very practical use. One lifts the tool up to the gutter, using the ring-shaped handle, places the solid sphere inside the gutter trough, and pushes out snow or other debris. This saves one from having to climb up on the roof.

An unusual invention for a toy is presented in Fig. 5.4. This is the "imaginary pet." The idea is that you could "walk" the imaginary pet much like the way you would walk an actual dog. Since the toy rolls, you don't have to hold it up. The original conception for the design was a toy that a blind person could use, perhaps as a substitute for a cane. I suspect that young children would also enjoy using it.

A interesting addition to the home is the "omnidirectional couch," shown in Fig. 5.5. This allows people to sit in any direction. The top part of the large sphere is made of soft material; you sit at the top and rest your feet on the surrounding ring. Or, you could also sit on the ring and lean back against the soft sphere.

A novel idea is the "snow vacuum," shown in Fig. 5.6. It is similar in concept to a vacuum cleaner; a vacuum is created inside the sphere, and snow is sucked up through the tube. Then, the snow is allowed to melt, and the water can be drained back out the tube. (Compare this invention to the "gutter cleaner" in Fig. 5.3, which was constructed out of the same parts and under the same functional restrictions.)

Finally, in Fig. 5.7, we have a "stove fire extinguisher," a useful addition to the kitchen. The unit is attached to the ceiling above the stove, using a retractable wire cable. If a stove fire breaks out, one can extinguish the fire by pulling the unit down and smothering it with the open half sphere, without having to use chemical sprays. I can certainly think of times when I wish I had one.

I also provide some examples of interesting inventions that were classified as "creative," but not "highly creative." Figure 5.8 presents the "bladed flashlight," a weapon that someone could use after dark. A sharp blade extends from the light source, which enables one to see exactly where the weapon is pointing. Such a weapon would be of value to policemen, for example.

The "seismic sphere," a device for detecting earthquakes, is shown in Fig. 5.9. The elevated, weighted sphere oscillates whenever the ground shakes, amplifying the ground vibrations. A motion-sensitive alarm can be placed inside the tubular chamber, alerting one to an impending quake. The interesting feature of the device is that it would pick up vertical as well as lateral ground movements, since the sphere is free to "bob" in every direction.

A very practical invention is the "solar heater," shown in Fig. 5.10. Solar heat is collected inside the transparent dome, as a consequence of the "greenhouse" effect. Solar cells then operate a simple fan, which blows the collected heat out through the vent.

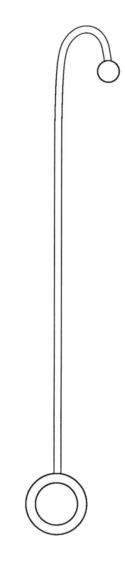

FIG. 5.3. The "gutter cleaner," constructed using the RING, TUBE and SPHERE, under the restriction that it had to be "a tool for removing snow." One lifts the tool and places the round end into a gutter to push out snow and other debris.

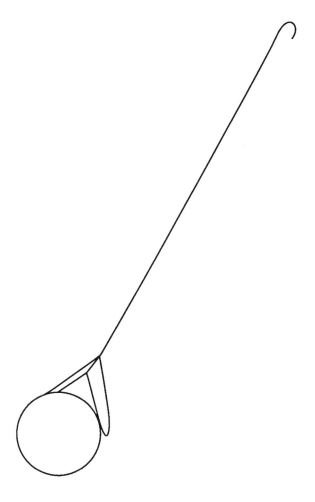

FIG. 5.4. The "imaginary pet," constructed using the WIRE, SPHERE, and BRACKET, under the restriction that it had to be "a game that a blind person would enjoy." The person could "walk" the toy, in place of using a cane.

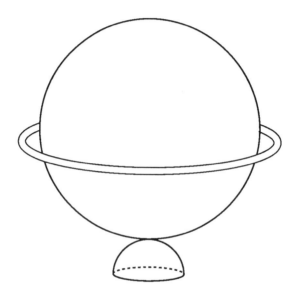

FIG. 5.5. The "omnidirectional couch," constructed using the RING, SPHERE, and HALF SPHERE, under the restriction that it had to be "a piece of furniture that you would enjoy looking at." The sphere is made of a soft material, and the ring serves as a surrounding foot rest.

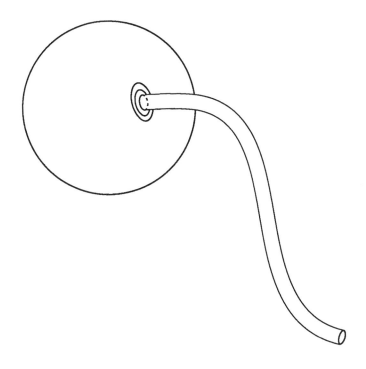

FIG. 5.6. A "snow vacuum," constructed using the RING, TUBE, and SPHERE, under the restriction that it had to be "a tool for removing snow." A vacuum is created inside the sphere, which sucks in the snow through the tube; the snow is then allowed to melt, and water is released back out though the tube. Compare to Figure 5.3, which presents a different invention constructed out of the same parts and under the same restrictions.

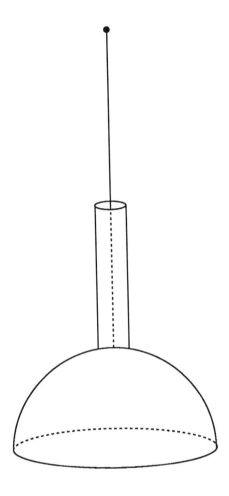

FIG. 5.7. A "stove fire extinguisher," constructed using the HALF SPHERE, TUBE, and WIRE, under the restriction that it had to be "an appliance that would help you cook dinner." If dinner turns into a stove fire, one simply pulls the appliance down using the retractable wire cable, and smothers the fire with the open half sphere.

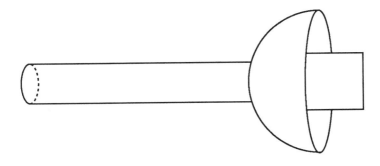

FIG. 5.8. The "bladed flashlight," constructed using the FLAT SQUARE, CYLINDER, and HALF SPHERE, under the restriction that it had to be "a weapon that uses light." A sharp blade extends from the light source, enabling one to see, at night, what the weapon is pointed at.

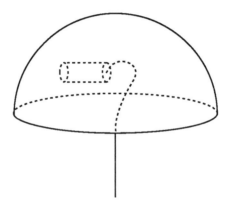

FIG. 5.9. The "seismic sphere," constructed using the HALF SPHERE, TUBE, and HOOK, under the restriction that it had to be "a device that measures earthquakes." Ground vibrations in all directions are amplified as the weighted sphere oscillates; a vibration-sensitive alarm is placed inside the tube to detect an impending quake.

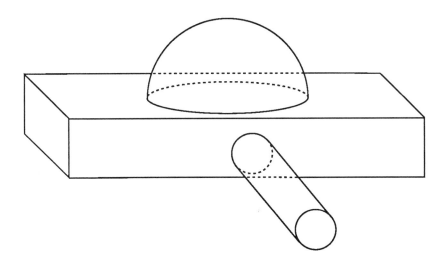

FIG. 5.10. A "solar heater," constructed using the HALF SPHERE, CYLINDER, and RECTANGULAR BLOCK, under the restriction that it had to be "an appliance that would heat your home." The transparent dome collects solar heat, while solar cells inside the unit operate a fan to blow the heat through the vent.

TABLE 5.5
Examples of Sets of Parts Used in Experiments on Creative
Invention in Which Object Types and Functions Were Restricted

1.	SPHERE SPHERE RECTANGULAR BLOCK	6.	WIRE FLAT SQUARE RING
2.	CUBE WIRE CYLINDER	7.	SPHERE CYLINDER TUBE
3.	CONE BRACKET CONE	8.	SPHERE CONE HOOK
4.	HALF SPHERE TUBE TUBE	9.	CUBE FLAT SQUARE RECTANGULAR BLOCK
5.	TUBE RING SPHERE	10.	HALF SPHERE RECTANGULAR BLOCK CUBE

READER PARTICIPATION:
SPECIALIZED INVENTIONS

Table 5.5 provides readers with an opportunity to try out either of these more restrictive invention tasks. Using the sets of parts provided in this table, try imagining an invention that conforms to one of the specific object types or functions listed in Tables 5.1 and 5.2. See if you notice any differences in how easily the two tasks can be performed.

SUMMARY

Restricting the object types and functions have different consequences for how successfully these techniques can be used to discover creative inventions. Whereas both restrictions reduce the overall number of practical inventions that subjects report, restricting the object functions does not reduce the number of creative inventions, in contrast to restricting the object types. Apparently, specifying the types of objects restricts too narrowly the kinds of features that the inventions must have.

THEORETICAL IMPLICATIONS

In the previous chapter, I concluded that restricting the parameters of the invention task, particularly the object parts and categories, increased the creative quality of the inventions. The present experiments show that this general principle must be qualified. Restricting the parameters does help, but only up to a point. The inventions cannot be restricted so severely that the parts one is given become altogether inappropriate. Evidently, this is what happened in Experiment 4, where the inventions had to conform to particular types of objects. The creative invention techniques can still be used in such cases, but the likelihood of being successful on any particular trial is reduced.

There are other possible ways of restricting the inventions, as suggested by various studies on concept formation. For example, one could try to restrict the characteristic features of an object category, as opposed to its "defining" features (e.g., Smith & Medin, 1981; Smith, Shoben, & Rips, 1974). Or, one could systematically restrict an object's features using the method of "attribute listing" (e.g., Adams, 1974). I would suspect, however, than any method that restricts the general category or function of an object would improve the creative potential of these techniques, whereas any method that restricts the specific types of objects would reduce their creative potential.

As a final note, many of the creative inventions reported here, as in the previous experiments, were somewhat "schematic," in that they would require some further refinement in order to be completely functional. The imagined forms seemed to capture the essential concept or idea underlying the invention, leaving one to fill in the details later on. Yet, this is often the nature of creative insight.

6

Preinventive Object Forms

Subjects in creative invention experiments typically report that they prefer to first imagine possible forms that could be made out of the parts and then consider possible interpretations of the forms. As in the earlier experiments on creative patterns, this "trial-and-error" strategy seems to be the more natural approach to the task, rather than trying to make the parts conform to some initial idea or preconception. In the present chapter, I explore some important implications of the notion that creative inventions can best be discovered only after a general form is constructed.

THE CONCEPT OF "PREINVENTIVE FORMS"

I shall begin by introducing the concept of a "Preinventive Form." These forms are the products of the "combinational play" of mental imagery. Initially, they represent interesting shapes and structures that seem potentially useful only in a general sense. Preinventive forms may then be interpreted as specific objects or concepts according to the demands of the situation or task. Thus, by considering preinventive forms and their implications, one may come to discover inventions that might not otherwise be conceived. In this respect, preinventive forms lead to inventive insights, not the other way around.

This suggests that in the creative invention experiments, it might be possible for people to do the task in the following way: They would first generate a specific preinventive form, without knowing how the form is supposed to be used. Then, they would be given the name of an object category, and they would have to interpret their preinventive form as some kind of invention within that category.

This would structure the task according to what appears to be the most natural way to discover the creative inventions.

It would also enable one to separate, experimentally, creative combinations of the parts from creative interpretations of the resulting forms. This is because the nature of the interpretations would be specified only after the preinventive forms were mentally constructed. The problem of how to separate creative synthesis from creative interpretation had been considered at the end of Chapter 3, in the context of creative pattern recognitions, but was not resolved by the methods for generating creative inventions in any of the previous experiments.

Note, also, that in the previous experiments on creative invention, subjects could have generated preinventive forms freely, changing them at will, according to their initial successes or failures at trying to interpret them. Thus, they might have discounted potentially useful forms by abandoning them prematurely. In the experiments to be reported next, subjects were always committed to a particular preinventive form.

PILOT EXPERIMENT: GENERATING PREINVENTIVE FORMS

I originally conceived of these experiments after informally attempting the earlier tasks. I noticed that many of the preinventive forms I had come up with would stick in my mind with a curious tenaciousness—like a haunting image, they would not go away. There was a compelling quality to them, something which I felt was very important, but which I could not really explain. And then, I would suddenly see the form as a particular kind of invention, and its "meaning" would become immediately clear. Could naive undergraduate students be taught to use this same technique of trying to interpret their preinventive forms? And if so, how well would it work compared with the procedures used in the previous experimental conditions, where subjects were not obliged to imagine preinventive forms?

In an initial pilot experiment, 23 subjects attempted to generate preinventive forms after being given three randomly chosen parts. They were told that they were to try to mentally assemble the parts to make "an interesting, potentially useful object." It was emphasized that they were not to make a specific object, like a chair or an appliance or a toy, but rather to try to come up with an interesting shape that might be useful in some general way. They were then given 1 minute to do so, with their eyes closed. At the end of the generation period, they were instructed to open their eyes and to draw the form if they had been able to come up with one. As in the previous experiments, additional instructions described the parts and explained how they could be combined.

There were 6 trials per subject, for a total of 138 trials. In all, the subjects were able to come up with a preinventive form on 136, or 98.6% of these trials;

thus, they were obviously able to do the task. Evidently, the 1-minute generation period provided sufficient time for all of the subjects to generate their preinventive forms.

Examples of some of the preinventive forms are given in Fig. 6.1. These forms seemed quite intriguing, suggesting that there was an invention of some kind "behind" them, waiting to be discovered.

INTERPRETING THE PREINVENTIVE FORMS
(EXPERIMENTS 6–7)

I then expanded the pilot experiment to give subjects an opportunity to interpret their preinventive forms according to particular object categories. There were two versions of the experiment.

In Experiment 6, a new group of 60 subjects were asked to generate preinventive forms at the beginning of each trial, exactly as subjects in the pilot experiment had done. They, too, were given 1 minute to produce the forms in imagination, then they were instructed to draw the forms on a response sheet. After doing this, the experimenter named one of the 8 object categories that had been used in the first three experiments on creative invention (see again Chapter 4). Again, the category names were randomly selected on each trial. The subjects were then told to inspect the object they had just drawn, and to try to interpret it as some kind of practical invention or device belonging to that category. They were given 1 minute to do so; then they were to name the object and describe it. Restricting the generation and interpretation periods to 1 minute each was done to equate the total "processing" time with that of the previous experiments, which had been 2 minutes. As before, there were 6 trials per subject, and naive experimenters were used.

The design of Experiment 7 was similar, except that the subjects were to use preinventive forms that other subjects had already generated. This was done to further examine the distinction between generating the forms and interpreting them as inventions. The procedure consisted of two steps.

First, a group of 60 subjects were asked to generate the preinventive forms, exactly as in the first part of Experiment 6. Then, another group of 60 subjects were given the response sheets for these subjects, on which their preinventive forms were drawn. Before the actual purpose of the experiment was disclosed, however, the new subjects were asked to rate each of the drawings, using a 5-point scale. First, they were told to rate the quality of the drawings, which meant how neatly the objects were drawn. Then, they rated what they felt was the potential usefulness of the depicted objects, apart from how well the objects were drawn. Quality of drawing and potential usefulness were therefore to be considered independently. For each rating, a score of "5" denoted the highest score; this corresponded to "Very Nicely Drawn" and "Potentially Very Useful"

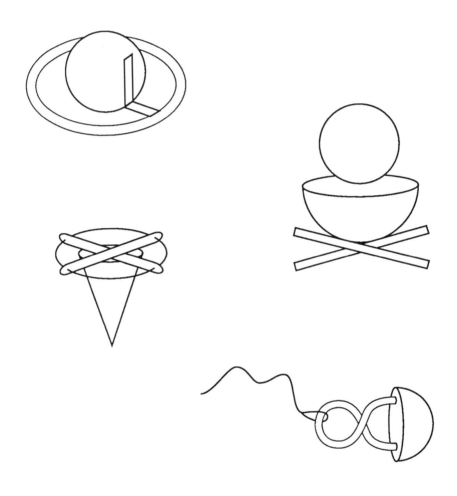

FIG. 6.1. Examples of "preinventive forms."

for the two scales, respectively. To make sure the subjects could identify the parts in the drawings, the experimenter named each of the parts before the ratings were made. Also, the experimenter explained that the parts could be made out of any material, and described the allowable ways in which the parts could be combined.

Including these rating scales served two purposes. First, it allowed us to assess whether the subjects' success at using other people's preinventive forms might depend on how well the forms were drawn, or on how useful the forms might seem. Whereas subjects who generate the preinventive forms would try to make them interesting and potentially useful to themselves, this doesn't mean that they would be perceived that way by others. Second, it gave the subjects an opportunity to become familiar with the forms before being asked to interpret them.

After the ratings were collected, the subjects participated in the interpretation phase of the experiment. As in Experiment 6, an object category was randomly chosen and named, and the subjects were given 1 minute to try to interpret the forms as some kind of practical invention or device belonging to that category. They were then to name the invention and describe it on the response sheets that had been provided with the drawings. If the previous subjects had not been able to come up with a form, they were to leave the spaces blank. This, however, occurred on only 2 of the 360 trials.

RESULTS OF THE EXPERIMENTS

How would subjects in these experiments do compare to those in the previous experiments? Consider, for example, Experiment 6, where subjects generated their own preinventive forms before they were given the category names. How would these subjects compare with those, say, in Experiment 2 of Chapter 4, where the subjects knew the category name before they imagined possible combinations of the parts?

One might expect, quite naturally, that Experiment 6 would be a much harder task, since the subjects would have no idea what it is they are supposed to invent when they start out. Instead, they must first commit themselves to a preinventive form, and then interpret it according to an arbitrarily chosen category, which they learn of only after the form is composed. Consider, however, the counterintuitive notion that these subjects might actually do better! Perhaps by forcing them to be committed to a particular preinventive form, the subjects would discover inventive possibilities that they might have overlooked, had they had the complete freedom to restructure the form to accommodate the category.

As Table 6.1 shows, Experiment 6, where subjects had generated and then interpreted their own preinventive forms, was the most successful experiment in the entire study: It yielded the greatest number of creative inventions (65), the greatest number of highly creative inventions (26), the highest proportion of practical inventions that were judged as creative (54.2%), and the highest propor-

TABLE 6.1
Number of Practical, Creative, and Highly Creative Inventions
Reported by Subjects According to Whether or Not They Used
Their Own Preinventive Forms (Experiments 6–7)

	Condition	
Type of Invention	Preinventive Forms Generated	Preinventive Forms Provided
Practical	120	69
Creative	65	20
Highly Creative	26	2

Note: The above categorizations are based on a total of 720 trials, 360 for each condition. "Creative" inventions were practical inventions rated as original; "Highly Creative" inventions received the highest possible rating on both practicality and originality.

tion of creative inventions that were judged as highly creative (40.0%). In addition, it had the highest proportion of subjects who generated at least one creative invention, as two-thirds of the subjects (66.7%) were able to do so. Evidently, the structure of this experiment created the ideal conditions for discovering creative inventions.

In comparing Experiments 6 and 7, there were highly significant differences in all measures of performance, as shown again in Table 6.1. When subjects generated their own preinventive forms, they came up with significantly more practical inventions, $\chi^2 (1) = 13.76$, $p < .001$, more creative inventions, $\chi^2 (1) = 23.82$, $p < .001$, and more highly creative inventions, $\chi^2 (1) = 20.57$, $p < .001$. Subjects in Experiment 7 produced only 20 inventions that were judged as creative, and only 2 of these were judged as highly creative.

Again, there was no effect of the order of experimental trials on the number of practical or creative inventions that subjects generated in either of the experiments (for all χ^2 tests, $p > .05$). This argues against the possibility that subjects simply learned to create better preinventive forms with practice. More importantly, it argues that subjects in Experiment 6 were not simply refining their preinventive forms across trials after having had practice in interpreting them.

The subjects' ratings in Experiment 7 indicated that the creative interpretations could not be attributed to the quality of the drawings or the initially perceived usefulness of the forms. These ratings did not distinguish whether the practical inventions that were later derived from the forms were judged as creative or noncreative (all $\chi^2 < 1$). Also, the fact that subjects in Experiment 7 generated a lower percentage of highly creative forms among those judged as creative, compared with subjects in Experiment 6, further argues against the possibility that these subjects did worse simply because they had difficulty understanding the drawings.

IMPLICATIONS OF THE RESULTS

These results have at least three immediate implications: They suggest, first of all, that it is better to commit yourself to using a preinventive form that seems potentially useful in some general sense, and then to explore its possibilities once an object category is selected, as the preferred strategy for coming up with creative inventions. Knowing the category in advance, and freely altering the preinventive form to conform to the category, may not lead one down the most creative paths.

Second, the successful use of this technique evidently depends on whether or not you use your own preinventive forms. Perhaps, in putting the forms together yourself, you develop a better "feel" for the forms and can more clearly see their potential applications. Or, perhaps there is a greater degree of personal involvement and commitment when using your own forms. In addition, the forms people generate themselves would more likely be relevant to their own past experiences. Thus, the preinventive forms that a person constructs might not be useful or inspiring to others.

This conclusion is further supported by the subjects' ratings of the potential usefulness of the forms in Experiment 7. These ratings were not terribly high (3.24 for the noncreative inventions and 2.85 for the creative inventions), suggesting that the experimental subjects found these preinventive forms overall to be less interesting and potentially useful than those that they would have generated themselves.

Third, the results imply that there is more to coming up with creative inventions than simply applying creative interpretations to a form. In Experiment 7, subjects were also provided with creative combinations of parts, but they were not able to interpret the parts with the same success as when they had generated their own preinventive forms. Again, there seems to be something special about preinventive forms that one generates for oneself; something that is suited to the individual, and that inspires further exploration.

EXAMPLES OF CREATIVE INVENTIONS

Examples of some of the highly creative inventions from Experiment 6 are presented next; a complete list of the creative inventions in Experiments 6 and 7 is provided in Table 6.2. All of the creative inventions reported in these experiments were unique.

In Fig. 6.2, there is a design for a "bread warmer." Electrical current from the wire heats the hollow metal cylinder and allows one to keep a loaf of bread warm without having to place it in the oven. The handle allows the appliance to be easily transported.

The "contact lens remover" is presented in Fig. 6.3. One places the rubber

TABLE 6.2
List of Inventions Classified as Creative and Highly Creative
(Experiments 6–7)

animal shelf	MUSICAL SPHERES
automatic plant waterer	* nail puller
ball catcher	pastry cooker
block ball toss	pie crust poker
* BREAD WARMER	playground arch
bug snatcher	* pogo ball
cone atomizer	pogo box
cone buoy	* POGO PLOP
conical grater	portable centrifuge
conical plant stand	portable cooler
* CONTACT LENS REMOVER	portable juicer
covered garden logs	quarters table
cross lamp	ring grenade
depth finder	* ring roller
diagonal cheese cutter	rolling ceiling lamp
egg holder	* rolling magazine rack
expanding vase	* rolling seeder
EYEBALL RAFT	* rolling tenderizer
* FAN HUMIDIFIER	rotating buffer
flexible lamp	* rotating seed planter
* FLEXIBLE PAPERWEIGHT	ROTATING SPEAKER STAND
food transport	screw remover
food washer	shoe organizer
four-way funnel	* sink unclogger
hammer assister	sliding hook
hand piercer	* SLIDING TOWEL HANGER
hand plow	* sliding wire noose
* hanging cutting board	* slope gauge
hanging plant holder	spherical grinder
* heat sensor	* swimmer buoy
heater cup	swing punching bag
hooked bottle opener	* TEETER TODDLER
* HUMIDITY DETECTOR	* TENSION WIND VANE
jewelry holder	toy equalizer
* juice tenderizer	tree carrier
* knife cleaner	tree house suite
laser surveyor	* tube filter
lint remover	* UNIVERSAL REACHER
locomotive storehouse	vaporizer separator
* MANUAL DISHWASHER	vegetable slicer
* measure mixer	water weigher
melting point indicator	weed cutter

Note: Creative inventions that were also classified as "Highly Creative" are denoted by an asterisk. The creative inventions that are described in the text are capitalized.

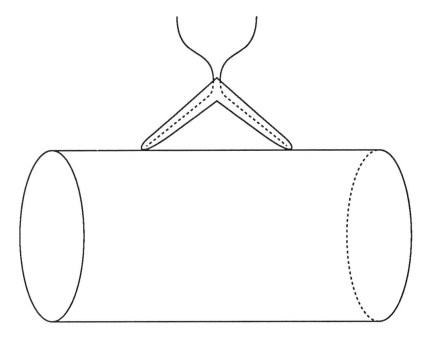

FIG. 6.2.　The "bread warmer," constructed using the WIRE, CYLINDER, and BRACKET. Electrical current from the wire heats the hollow metal cylinder, allowing one to keep a loaf of bread warm without having to place it in the oven.

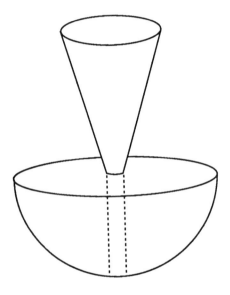

FIG. 6.3. The "contact lens remover," constructed using the HALF SPHERE, CONE, and TUBE. One places the rubber cone against the contact lens, covers the back of the tube with a finger, lifts the lens off the eye, and then removes the contact from the cone by releasing the finger from the tube.

cone against the contact lens, and covers the open tube with a finger. The lens is then lifted from the eye. By releasing the finger from the tube, the contact is then released for storage.

A simple design for a "fan humidifier" is shown in Fig. 6.4. One hangs the unit from the ceiling. The open cone is filled with water, which trickles down the wire and is turned into a mist by the rotating fan. The blowing spray humidifies the air.

The "flexible paperweight" is shown in Fig. 6.5. The tube connecting the weights can be bent to cover larger or smaller sheets of paper or portions of a desk. It also has a nice decorative feel.

In Fig. 6.6 there is a design for a "humidity detector." This instrument works by having a current pass through the wire while the cylinder and wire are rotated. The wire is thin and uninsulated, and is thus exposed to the humidity in the air, which affects its resistance. Changes in humidity can then be measured by recording changes in the current.

The "manual dishwasher" is presented in Fig. 6.7. The bracket attaches the unit above the sink, and the cylindrical sponge is lowered by a retractable wire support. The unique shape of the sponge enables one to easily clean such items as glasses and cups. And because the sponge is hung in the air, it can dry more easily.

A transportation novelty is the "pogo plop," shown in Fig. 6.8. The bottom part of the half sphere consists of a bouncy rubber. Two people stand on opposite sides of the cone, hold onto the hooked-shaped rod, and hop away. When the travelers are tired, the pogo plop converts to a chair; whereupon you sit on top of the half sphere, and rest your back against the cone. The hook lets you hang the device and use it as a swing.

The "sliding towel hanger" is shown in Fig. 6.9. The flat square is attached to the bathroom wall or ceiling, and the hanger slides along the wire, allowing one to move a towel, washcloth, or bathrobe to where they are easier to reach. This would be very useful, for example, when taking a shower.

Figure 6.10 presents a design for a "teeter toddler," which is a simple teeter totter that two infants can use. The half sphere allows the children to spin around as they rock up and down, and they can grasp the cylindrical post for security. Interestingly, a similar preinventive form was interpreted by another subject as a "rotating speaker stand," in which one places a set of speakers at opposite ends of the rectangular block, and then rotates the stand to achieve the best acoustical effects.

A clever invention is the "tension wind vane," shown in Fig. 6.11. The large hollow cylinder is made of a light material, and it attached to the cube by a continuous wire. The cube contains a tensionometer that records changes in the wire's tension when the wind blows on the cylinder. This provides information about changes in wind speed and direction.

A handy device is the "universal reacher," shown in Fig. 6.12. The wire is

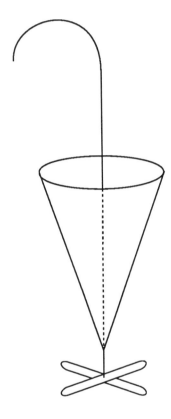

FIG. 6.4. The "fan humidifier," constructed using the HOOK, CONE, and CROSS. The unit is hung from the ceiling, the open cone is filled with water, and the water trickles down the wire and is turned into a fine mist by the rotating fan.

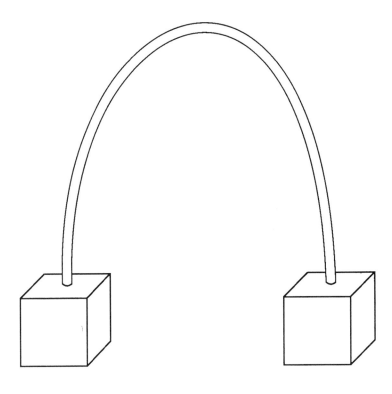

FIG. 6.5. The "flexible paperweight," constructed using the CUBE, TUBE, and CUBE. The tube connecting the weights can be bent to cover larger or smaller sheets of paper or portions of a desk.

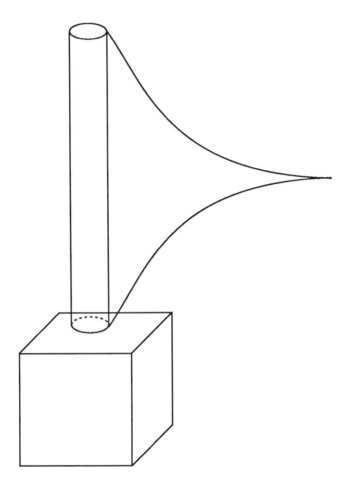

FIG. 6.6.   The "humidity detector," constructed using the CUBE, WIRE, and CYLINDER. A current passes through a thin, uninsulated wire that rotates together with the cylinder; the moisture content of the air affects the resistance of the wire, which provides a measure of the amount of humidity.

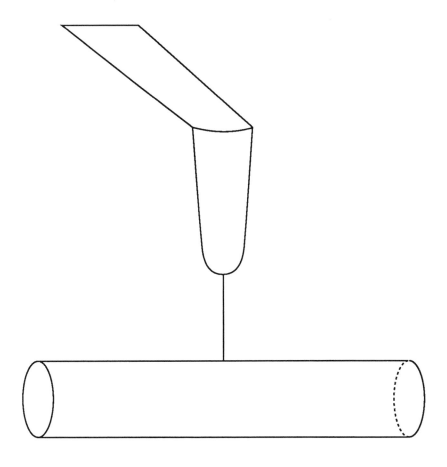

FIG. 6.7.   The "manual dishwasher," constructed using the WIRE, CYLINDER, and BRACKET. The cylindrical sponge, which can easily clean such items as glasses and cups, is lowered by a retractable wire.

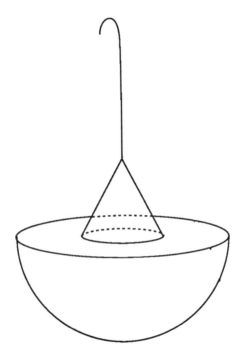

FIG. 6.8. The "pogo plop," constructed using the HALF SPHERE, HOOK, and CONE. The bottom part of the half sphere consists of a bouncy rubber; two people stand on opposite sides of the cone, hold onto the hooked-shaped rod, and hop away. By sitting on the half sphere, the pogo plop converts to a chair; the hook also enables one to use it as a swing.

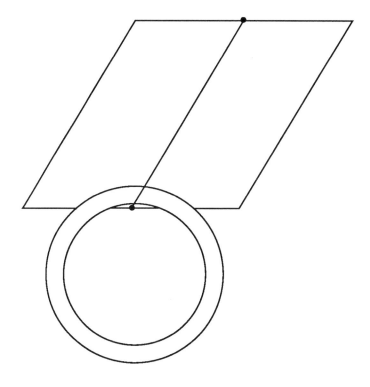

FIG. 6.9. The "sliding towel hanger," constructed using the WIRE, RING, and FLAT SQUARE. The flat square is attached to the bathroom wall or ceiling, and the hanger slides along the wire, allowing one to move towels, washcloths, or bathrobes to where they are easier to reach.

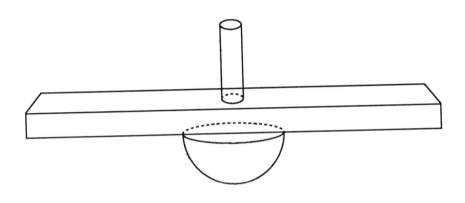

FIG. 6.10. The "teeter toddler," constructed using the CYLINDER, HALF SPHERE, and RECTANGULAR BLOCK. The half sphere allows young children to spin around as they use the toy as a teeter totter. The same preinventive form was also interpreted by another subject as a "rotating speaker stand," on which speakers are placed and then rotated to the ideal acoustical position.

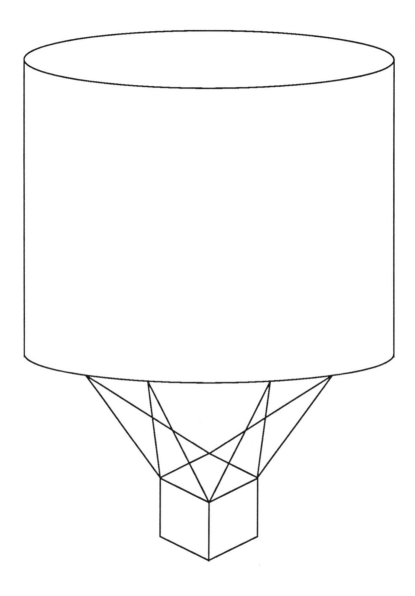

FIG. 6.11. The "tension wind vane," constructed using the CUBE, WIRE, and CYLIN-DER. The large hollow cylinder, which is made of a light material, is attached to the cube by a continuous wire. The cube contains a tensionometer that records changes in the wire's tension whenever the wind blows on the cylinder, providing information about changes in wind speed and direction.

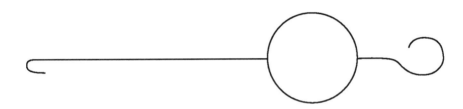

FIG. 6.12.   The "universal reacher," constructed using the HOOK, SPHERE, and WIRE. The wire is drawn out of the sphere and can be shaped and bent to retrieve things that fall into hard-to-reach places, while the hook allows the device to be secured.

drawn out of the sphere and can be shaped and bent to retrieve things that fall into hard-to-reach places. The hook allows the device to be secured so that both hands can be used to guide the wire.

Even some of the inventions that did not receive the very highest ratings are also worth mentioning; for example, the "eyeball raft," shown in Fig. 6.13. The half-sphere is made of plexiglass or other transparent material, and allows one to observe underwater life. The arms of the cross function as floating pontoons, and the cone provides a sheltered cover for the viewing area.

An example of a creative invention from Experiment 7 is shown in Fig. 6.14. This is the "musical spheres," a music box containing two metal balls. Each side of the box plays a different tune when the balls are in contact with it. You change the tune by simply turning the box.

As in the previous experiments, many of the subjects mentioned that they wanted to continue working on their inventions to refine them further. Their preinventive forms seemed to provide the basic insight into the essential structure or concept underlying the invention, which might then need some additional parts or slight modifications to actually function as desired.

READER PARTICIPATION: PREINVENTIVE FORMS

Tables 6.3 and 6.4 give readers a chance to explore the possibilities of their own preinventive forms. First, for each of the sets of parts listed in Table 6.3., try to imagine a preinventive form that would strike you as being interesting or potentially useful in designing something. Then, without looking yet at Table 6.4, record your preinventive forms.

Table 6.4 then provides a list of object categories to be used in conjunction with the sets of parts in Table 6.3. For each "trial," try to interpret your preinventive form as some kind of invention belonging to the designated category. As in the previous examples, the parts and categories have not been preselected, but represent how the experimental trials might actually occur. Note, also, how the preinventive forms give rise to the inventions; in particular, whether you had a sudden insight at the moment you discovered an invention that corresponded to the preinventive form.

SUMMARY

It might seem remarkable that untrained undergraduates can come into an experiment, be given a set of randomly chosen parts, generate preinventive forms without knowing what kind of invention the forms should correspond to, and then be able to interpret their preinventive forms as creative inventions. And, it might seem even more remarkable that this turns out to be the most successful condition of all. Subjects in the previous experiments came up with fewer creative

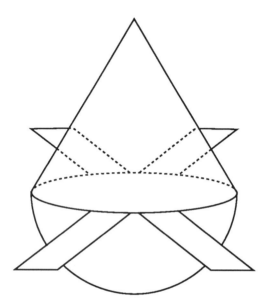

FIG. 6.13. The "eyeball raft," constructed using the HALF SPHERE, CROSS, and CONE. The transparent half sphere allows one to observe underwater life, the arms of the cross function as floating pontoons, and the cone provides a sheltered cover for the viewing area.

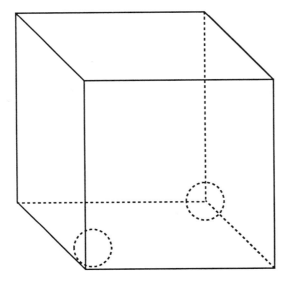

FIG. 6.14.   The "musical spheres," constructed using the SPHERE, CUBE, and SPHERE. Each side of the cube plays a different tune when the spheres fall in contact with it.

TABLE 6.3
Examples of Sets of Parts Used in Experiments on Generating
and Interpreting Preinventive Forms

1.	SPHERE RECTANGULAR BLOCK CONE		6.	FLAT SQUARE FLAT SQUARE WIRE
2.	HALF SPHERE SPHERE TUBE		7.	CYLINDER HOOK CUBE
3.	CUBE RING CUBE		8.	FLAT SQUARE SPHERE BRACKET
4.	TUBE WHEELS HOOK		9.	CUBE WIRE CYLINDER
5.	CONE CONE RECTANGULAR BLOCK		10.	WIRE RING FLAT SQUARE

Note: These sets of parts are to be used in conjunction with the object categories provided in Table 6.4, but only *after* the preinventive forms are generated.

inventions when they knew the category in advance, when they could choose their own category, or when they could choose their own parts. Yet, these results are consistent with the impressions subjects typically had when doing the earlier versions of the task—that it is better not to constrain the mental synthesis to conform to an initial idea or preconception. Rather, one should start out by considering an interesting preinventive form, and then commit oneself to interpreting the form within a general object category.

The present experiments show, further, that it is better to use preinventive forms that you generate yourself, rather than those that other people generate, which are likely to be less interesting or meaningful. Hence, the discovery of creative inventions is not simply a matter of coming up with clever interpretations of the preinventive forms. There has to be something special or natural about the forms themselves.

THEORETICAL IMPLICATIONS

There is another interesting difference between the creative inventions that subjects discovered when they were using their own preinventive forms, compared to when they were using the preinventive forms generated by someone else. I was struck by the almost "magical" quality of many of these inventions; they seemed so simple and elegant and natural. It's like the difference between a

TABLE 6.4
Examples of Object Categories That Were Randomly Paired
With Sets of Parts After the Preinventive Forms Were Generated

1.	PERSONAL ITEMS	6.	TOOLS AND UTENSILS
2.	FURNITURE	7.	SCIENTIFIC INSTRUMENTS
3.	WEAPONS	8.	TOOLS AND UTENSILS
4.	FURNITURE	9.	TRANSPORTATION
5.	TOYS AND GAMES	10.	FURNITURE

Note: These categories are to be used with the corresponding sets of parts listed in Table 6.3.

composer's original melody and variations on someone else's music; the composer's style might be apparent in the variations, but there would still be something missing in the overall composition. This is not to say that one could never discover a wonderful invention using another person's designs, but rather, that this could not be done arbitrarily. The design would have to be something that the person would have conceived of also.

It is also interesting to note how the preinventive forms seem to come "alive" when a person discovers what they should be. Until then, the forms merely seem "enchanting," such as those shown in Fig. 6.1. The experience one has in interpreting the preinventive forms is not unlike the way an archeologist might react, for example, after having discovered the function of an ancient artifact.

In fact, one experiences a curious illusion of "intentionality" when examining inventions that were derived from the preinventive forms: Even though the categories were specified only after the preinventive forms were constructed, one has the impression that the particular design was intended that way all along (as readers may have felt when inspecting the inventions presented in Figs. 6.2– 6.14). In other words, one feels as if the form were constructed to fit the invention concept, whereas it actually happened the other way around. This speaks to the broad inventive potential of the preinventive forms—once interpreted, it seems as if no other interpretation would properly fit the form; and yet, the assignment of categories to the preinventive forms was arbitrary.

In this regard, one might ask whether subjects in Experiment 6 might have designed their preinventive forms with a particular category in mind, which, by chance, just happened to match the actual category on certain trials. This possibility can be dismissed, however, for two reasons. First, such anticipations would only be correct on an average of one out of eight trials, since there were eight categories in all. Second, and more importantly, subjects were able to come up with more creative inventions than in those experiments where they actually knew the category in advance, and hence, where they would not need to guess or anticipate the category at all.

Another implication of these findings is that they argue against the possibility that subjects are merely responding to novel, random associations in coming up with their inventions—as, for example, one might do in creativity tasks where unrelated words or concepts are combined arbitrarily. That's not what's happening here. The preinventive forms are not simply random associations among parts. If they were, it wouldn't matter whether a person uses his or her own preinventive forms or somebody else's. Again, there is more to creative discovery than simply interpreting random events in a novel way.

The method of first generating and then interpreting preinventive forms is similar in some respects to the technique of "brainstorming," where people generate ideas freely and uncritically at first and then evaluate and interpret them later on (e.g., Adams, 1974; Osborn, 1953). However, brainstorming is usually employed to generate as many solutions as possible for trying to solve a particular problem. In contrast, preinventive forms should be considered as "universal" solutions to a wide range of potential problems, an idea I shall return to in Chapter 9.

Chapter
7

Personal Inventions

If the technique of generating and interpreting preinventive forms is as robust as the results of the previous chapter suggest, it should be possible for anyone to use the technique, at leisure, to come up with a virtually unlimited number of inventions. I therefore decided to put the technique to a personal test, to see whether I, too, could come up with new ideas for creative inventions using my own preinventive forms. I decided to do this under less formal conditions, where there were no time restrictions on interpreting the forms, in the hope that I might be able to discover a creative invention for each one of the forms.

Another reason why I wanted to explore these methods myself is that there is no guarantee that subjects in these experiments had never previously seen or thought about the creative inventions they reported. Although it seemed unlikely that this could explain the previous findings, given the sheer novelty of many of the inventions, and the surprise that subjects typically expressed upon having discovered them, it is always possible that a subject might have previously considered the invention somewhere before, and then simply "recognized" it again in the preinventive form. Since there is no way of ruling this out completely, short of knowing the experiential history of each subject, I decided to see for myself whether this technique could lead me to discover inventions that I knew I could not have conceived of at any previous time.

INFORMAL EXPLORATIONS

I began by doing the preinventive form task of Experiment 6 for a total of 48 trials, with the intention of coming up with a creative invention on every single trial. I first obtained a new list of randomly generated sets of parts, and allowed myself 1 minute to visualize a preinventive form for each set. Then, after I had recorded the preinventive forms, I had the computer randomly generate one of the object categories for each trial, and I attempted to interpret the preinventive form as a practical invention within that object category. Instead of restricting the interpretation time to 1 minute, as had been done in that experiment, I allowed myself as much time as I needed to interpret the form.

I quickly discovered that it was, in fact, possible to come up with interesting, even exciting interpretations for each of the preinventive forms, under these less restrictive conditions. The actual interpretation times ranged from less than 1 minute to a maximum of 15 minutes. Sometimes I would see the invention right away; other times I would have to think about something else temporarily, and then return to the preinventive form.

I noticed that the preinventive forms would often stick in my mind, even after my concentration had become fatigued. The experimental subjects had reported this, and it was indeed truly fascinating—as if the forms were "inviting" me to consider them further. I felt there were important inventions underlying the forms, but I never knew exactly what they were until the insight finally came—whereupon the meaning of the preinventive forms was suddenly clear. In the following section, I present examples of some of these personal inventions, and will try to describe what was going through my head as I was attempting to interpret the preinventive forms. A complete list of all of my inventions for the 48 trials is provided in Table 7.1.

EXAMPLES OF THE AUTHOR'S INVENTIONS

The first example of a preinventive form that I constructed is shown in Fig. 7.1; this was to be a toy or game. I thought about a bubble gum machine, but it didn't seem quite right. Then I visualized the object on top of a child's table, and imagined the child trying to get candy out of it, and it became a candy dispenser. But there was something preventing him from doing so. Then I realized that the candy dispenser had a mechanism that allowed the child to obtain only a limited amount of candy in a given day; some sort of timer or regulator that was contained in the base. Hence the preinventive form became a "controlled candy dispenser."

In the next example, shown in Fig. 7.2, the preinventive form was to be some kind of tool or utensil. I imagined rubbing the object between my hands, and mentally "observed" the spinning ring at the end. I then realized that the object was a "hand mixer," a utensil that could have many practical uses in kitchens and on camping trips.

For the preinventive form shown in Fig. 7.3, which was also to be a tool or utensil, my first reaction was that you could grab the handle and pound with it. But the purpose of the surrounding tube was perplexing. Then I imagined what might happen if I dropped the object. If it fell into the water it would float, and

TABLE 7.1
List of Inventions Generated by the Author

absorption gauge	mirror cosmetic
adjustable table base	NAIL GUIDE
air boat	portable aerometer
beam focuser	portable battering ram
buoy ball	portable park bench
child spinner	portable washbowl
cloud solarium	power plunger
compact sonar	PULL-UP SWING
compression air cleaner	REFRACTION VIEWER
cone sail	reversible photo displayer
CONTROLLED CANDY DISPENSER	rotating blade mixer
curtainless shower	rotating clothesline
elastic toestrap	sander level
hang spinner	SEDIMENT COIL
hanging bed platform	shield block game
hand masher	SPIRALING SLICER
HAND MIXER	SPRING-LOADED ANIMAL TRAP
hand-held clothes washer	twister mixer
HAND-HELD ICE BREAKER	UFO RING TOSS
ILLUMINATED HORS D'OEUVRE STAND	vacuum juicer
INFRARED FOOTREST	vibration bomb
MAGNIFYING FISH TANKS	wall-mounted coat rack
marble toss	WATCH ENLARGER
masher mixer	WOBBLE DETECTOR

Note: Inventions that are described in the text are capitalized.

that is why there was a miniature "life preserver" around it! I realized, at that point, that the tool had to be a "hand-held ice breaker."

The next preinventive form, shown in Fig. 7.4, was to be interpreted within the category "furniture." I envisioned the object standing up in the middle of my livingroom; it was illuminated, and very pretty. But what would belong in the cone? I thought of wanting food, and realized that the only acceptable possibility was *hors d'oeuvres,* such as pieces of candy or nuts. The illumination seemed appropriate; it would help you to see the hors d'oeuvres and would add to the attractiveness and novelty of the serving sphere. Hence, this became the "illuminated hors d'oeuvre stand."

The preinventive form in Fig. 7.5 was also to be interpreted as a piece of furniture. I immediately visualized placing my feet on top of the cube, underneath the cone "lamp." As I imagined that my feet were getting cold, I thought of putting a heating bulb in the lamp. The resulting invention is the "infrared footrest."

In Fig. 7.6, the preinventive form consisted of two spheres on top of a cube. I imagined seeing fish swimming around in the spheres, and the spheres turned into fishtanks. Then I imagined looking at the fishtanks from different viewing

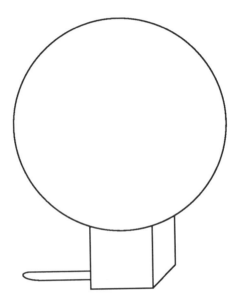

FIG. 7.1. The "controlled candy dispenser," constructed using the SPHERE, BRACKET, and CUBE. A counter limits how many pieces of candy a child can obtain in a given day. The dispenser functions much like a bubble gum machine, and can be mounted on a child's table or desk.

FIG. 7.2. The "hand mixer," constructed using the RING, CONE, and CYLINDER. One holds the handle between both hands and rubs it back and forth to mix ingredients or other substances.

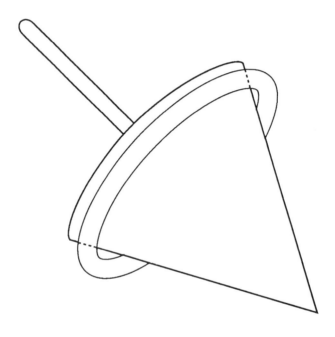

FIG. 7.3. The "hand-held ice breaker," constructed using the BRACKET, CONE, and TUBE. The cone is made of steel, and is used to pound holes in the ice. The surrounding rubber tube allows the tool to float if dropped in the water.

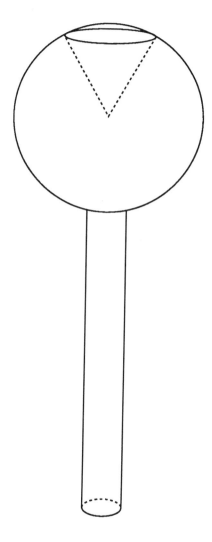

FIG. 7.4.   The "illuminated hors d'oeuvre stand," constructed using the SPHERE, CYL-INDER, and CONE. Hors d'oeuvres are placed in the cone; the sphere is transparent and is illuminated from below.

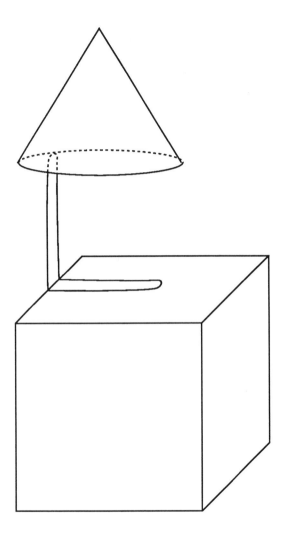

FIG. 7.5. The "infrared footrest," constructed using the CONE, CUBE, and BRACKET. The cone contains an infrared lamp to warm the feet.

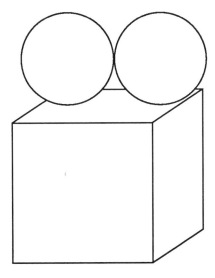

FIG. 7.6. The "magnifying fishtanks," constructed using the SPHERE, SPHERE, and CUBE. One fishtank functions as a giant lens to magnify the other when viewed from different angles.

perspectives, and noticed in my image that when one fishtank was positioned in front of the other, it served as a large lens, magnifying the fish in the tank behind it. This preinventive form thus became the "magnifying fishtanks."

The preinventive form in Fig. 7.7 had to be interpreted as a tool or utensil. I first imagined putting things inside of the cylindrical cavity, but this didn't make any sense. Then I imagined holding the object against a wall, with the cavity perpendicular to the wall surface. I thought of hammering a nail through the hole. Suddenly I realized what the tool was for. It was a "nail guide," allowing you to guide a nail without risking injury to your fingers! The cylindrical hole would be larger in diameter than the head of the nail, so that the guide could be easily removed once the nail was started. And, the tool could come in different sizes for different-sized nails.

A "toy or game" was the category of interpretation for the preinventive form shown in Fig. 7.8. I imagined a child sitting inside the elastic loop, which was hung from a tree by the hook. The child was swinging, holding onto the bars formed by the cross at the top. But what was the purpose of the bars? I then imagined the child swinging toward an obstacle on the ground. By pulling himself up on the swing, he was able to avoid the collision. So this preinventive form became the "pull-up swing."

The preinventive form in Fig. 7.9 was to be a "scientific instrument." At first I had no idea what kind of device this could be. I imagined putting small objects inside the cube and illuminating them, as if it were some kind of microscope. But it didn't quite "feel" like a microscope. Then I imagined looking at the cone from the side and mentally "seeing" the entire contents of the cube as the light from below was refracted by the cone. The instrument was, obviously, a "refraction viewer."

Coming up with a "tool or utensil" for the object shown in Fig. 7.10 would be a real challenge, as I had put together a rather unusual preinventive form. I imagined forcing water through the coiled tube, and I mentally watched the coils. With clear water, nothing happened. Then I imagined forcing dirty water through the tube, and discovered that the sediment in the water would collect at the bottom of the coils! This was, consequently, a "sediment coil." To remove the sediment, simply take out the flexible tube and straighten it.

I discovered a new type of utensil while mentally exploring the preinventive form shown in Fig. 7.11. I imagined taking this object and placing it on top of something that needed to be sliced, as the bracket reminded me of a cutting blade. I then realized that by rotating the object, and applying mild pressure, you could obtain thin, continuous slices of meat, cheese, or whatever it was you were cutting. The utensil would "spiral" its way through the food, and was thus a "spiraling slicer."

A type of "weapon" was the category for the preinventive form shown in Fig. 7.12. While mentally exploring this form, I imagined the wheels spinning around

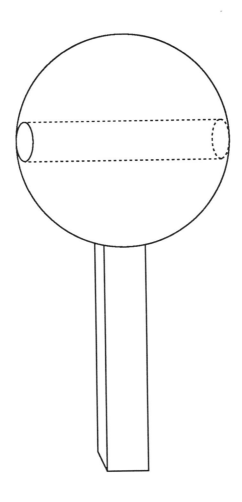

FIG. 7.7. The "nail guide," constructed using the CYLINDER, SPHERE, and RECTAN-GULAR BLOCK. Used to support and guide a nail while hammering, without risking injury to the fingers.

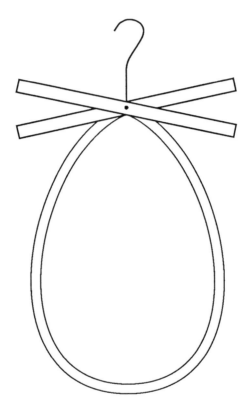

FIG. 7.8. The "pull-up swing," constructed using the TUBE, HOOK, and CROSS. The child sits inside the elastic loop and swings, while pulling him- or herself up using the bars on the cross.

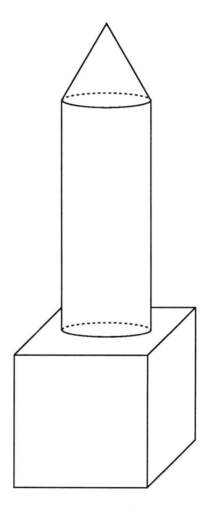

FIG. 7.9. The "refraction viewer," constructed using the CONE, CUBE, and CYLINDER. The glass cone refracts light from below, providing a panoramic view of the contents of the cube.

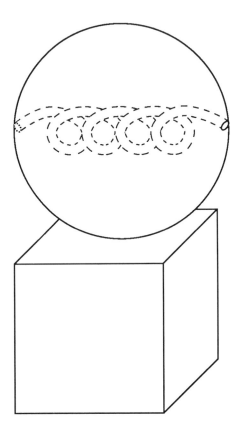

FIG. 7.10. The "sediment coil," constructed using the CUBE, TUBE, and SPHERE. Liquid is forced through the coil and sediment collects at the bottom of the coil loops; the coil can then be removed and straightened to remove the sediment.

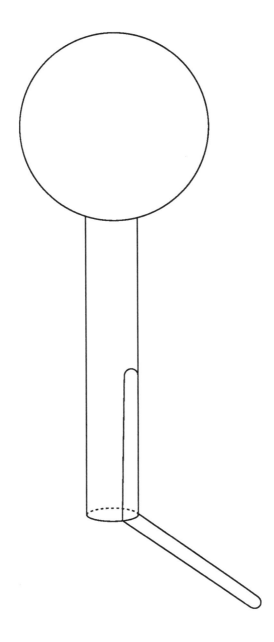

FIG. 7.11. The "spiraling slicer," constructed using the CYLINDER, SPHERE, and BRACKET. You place the utensil on meat or cheese, and as you press down and rotate the handle the blade slices thin, continuous layers.

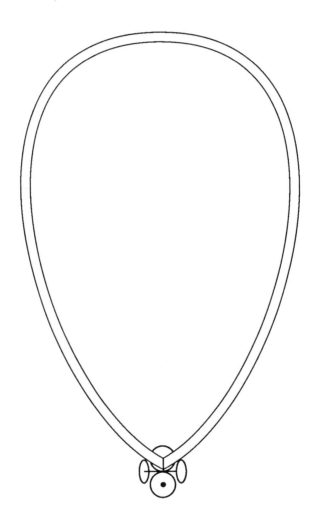

FIG. 7.12. The "spring-loaded animal trap," constructed using the TUBE, WHEELS, and WHEELS. The wheels are under spring tension; when an animal steps inside the loop, the mechanism releases and the loop is tightened around the animal's legs, without harming the animal.

rapidly—this caused the loop to twist itself together. It was then obvious how this "weapon" worked. You wind up the wheels, using a spring or other tension-producing device, and place the loop flat on the ground. When a person steps inside the loop, the tension on the wheels is released and the loop winds tightly around the person's legs. But then I realized that this same device could be used to trap animals without harming them. It became, appropriately, the "spring-loaded animal trap."

A "toy or game" was the category for the next preinventive form, shown in Fig. 7.13. I imagined a game in which the ring-shaped tube could be thrown like a frisbee, and the object of the game was to have the tube land on top of the hemispherical post. Then I imagined the tube glowing, like a UFO, and realized that this game was to be played at night. The hemispheres on the posts were illuminated, like "landing pads," and you pretended that the rings were flying saucers trying to land. I called the game the "UFO ring toss."

The preinventive form in Fig. 7.14 had to be interpreted as a "personal item." I imagined placing various things on the hook, like keys and clothing. When I imagined hanging my watch there, I suddenly realized what this was for. The large hemisphere in front of the watch was a clear lens, and this served to magnify the watch face so that you could use your watch as a clock when it wasn't being worn. This "watch enlarger" could be mounted on a desk or dresser.

Finally, I present a curious preinventive form in Fig. 7.15, which had to be interpreted as a "scientific instrument." I first imagined placing the object on top of a table. It wobbled. I then realized that if the table wobbled, even slightly, the object would also wobble and the vibrations would be amplified at the top of the shaft, where the metal ring was located. Motion of the ring could then be detected electronically or by using a light source. Thus, the form became a "wobble detector."

I can swear (on my favorite bicycle) that I had never thought of any of these inventions before. They were as much a surprise to me as they might have been to you or anyone else. Indeed, my experiences in interpreting these preinventive forms was reminiscent of the kinds of image discoveries reported by Kekulé and others that were considered at the beginning of this book.

Many of the properties of the preinventive forms that I "noticed" while visualizing them can be considered "emergent" properties as described in Chapters 2 and 3; that is, they were not apparent when the image was first formed. In particular, the preinventive forms would often reveal new properties as I visualized the consequences of spinning, turning, and dropping them. The notion that the dynamic characteristics of an object often help one to identify the object has been supported by many recent studies (e.g., Freyd, 1987; Johansson, 1975; Shepard, 1981, 1984).

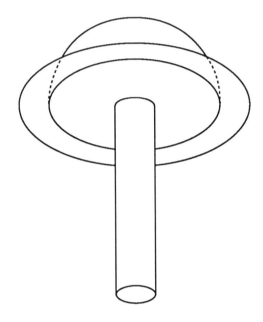

FIG. 7.13. The "UFO ring toss," constructed using the TUBE, HALF SPHERE, and CYLINDER. The hemispherical landing "post" has an illuminated top; the tube rings are flourescent and glow in the dark as they are spun toward the post.

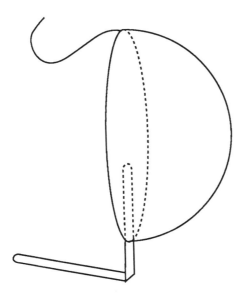

FIG. 7.14. The "watch enlarger," constructed using the BRACKET, HOOK, and HALF SPHERE. Mounted on a desk or dresser, the enlarger has a hook from which you hang your watch. The watch face is enlarged, and this lets your watch function as a clock when not being worn.

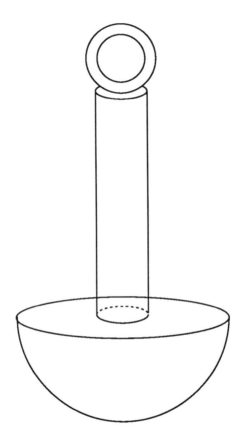

FIG. 7.15. The "wobble detector," constructed using the CYLINDER, RING, and HALF SPHERE. The device is placed on the ground or other flat surface; slight wobbles are amplified by the extension and are detected electronically or optically using the metal ring at the top.

SPONTANEOUS CREATIVE INVENTIONS

One day I was describing the concept of preinventive forms to one of my classes. While they were attempting to construct their own preinventive forms, I had a particularly vivid image of the form that is reproduced in Fig. 7.16. As I started to consider this image, I recalled that I had recently allowed my sink to overflow after having left the water running. I then had the classic "aha" reaction—this was a design for a "safety drain plug"! To close the drain, you stretch the elastic tube and secure it to the top of the sink or bathtub; the rubber ball will be pressed against the underside of the drain hole. The drain will then remain closed until the weight of the water exceeds the elastic force of the tube, whereupon the drain will open and the excess water will escape. The more water that enters, the more the drain opens. This prevents accidental overspills.

As another example of a spontaneous invention, one day I happened to think of the preinventive form shown in Fig. 7.17. I had no idea what it could be; it just struck me as an interesting form. Then I imagined seeing it in a back yard, where a swimming pool might be found. I could visualize children swimming in either of the square "pools," and then realized that the hemispherical top could serve as a transparent "bridge," allowing the children to climb from one pool to the other. This "pool bridge" would be warmed by the sun, providing a warm place to rest while transferring between pools.

One thing I noticed about all of these preinventive forms is that they initially impressed me as being mysterious, intriguing, and potentially meaningful in some abstract sense, but then came to life only after the interpretation was found. In this sense, the preinventive forms were "reified" by the interpretations. Also, I felt that each of the interpretations seemed intuitively "obvious" in retrospect, and that it was difficult to conceive of the preinventive forms as having been anything else.

STUDENT INVENTIONS

I also had several of my students attempt to use these same techniques to come up with their own inventions, giving them extended time to interpret their preinventive forms. Like myself, these students were able to come up with an invention of some kind on every trial, and reported that they were often "surprised" at the sudden recognition of potential uses of the preinventive forms they had created. I provide several examples of these students' inventions:

One student, Traci Ratliff, discovered a "salad tosser," shown in Fig. 7.18. Salad fixings are placed in the sphere, which is shook to toss the salad. One then pours the mixed salad into bowls by turning the tosser over and guiding it with the bracket.

Traci also discovered several other inventions that I would like to mention. The "sliding ceiling lamp," shown in Fig. 7.19, allows overhead illumination to

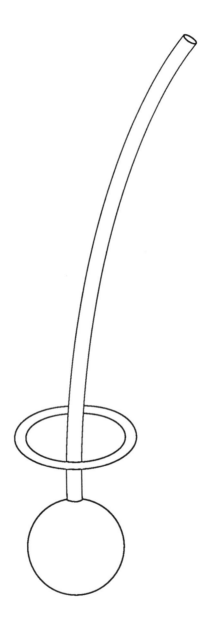

FIG. 7.16. The "safety drain plug," constructed using the SPHERE, RING, and TUBE. The tube is elastic and holds the rubber sphere against the drain hole until the weight of the water exceeds the elastic force of the tube, whereupon the drain opens and the excess water escapes.

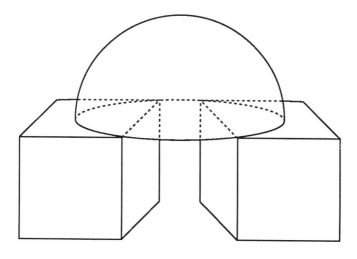

FIG. 7.17. The "pool bridge," constructed using the CUBE, CUBE, and HALF SPHERE. The transparent half sphere functions as a "bridge" connecting the two pools, allowing children to climb from one pool to the other.

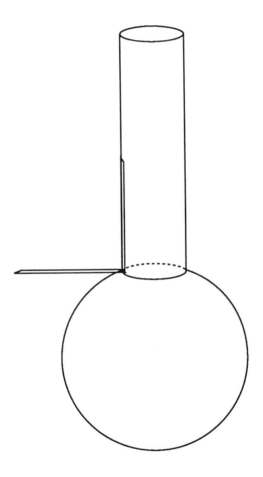

FIG. 7.18. The "salad tosser," constructed using the SPHERE, BRACKET, and CYLIN-
DER. Salad fixings are placed in the sphere, which is shook to toss the salad; one then
pours the salad into bowls by turning the tosser over and guiding it with the bracket.

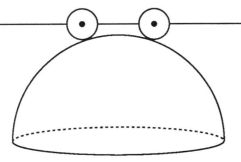

FIG. 7.19. The "sliding ceiling lamp," constructed using the HALF SPHERE, WIRES, and WHEELS. The overhead lamp can be moved to illuminate different parts of a room or house.

be moved to different parts of a room or house, as needed. The "adjustable playground," shown in Fig. 7.20, is particularly intriguing. Children climb up into the transparent dome and slide down the tube, which can be repositioned in various ways.

Another student, Donna McKeown, discovered the "basketball dribbler," shown in Fig. 7.21. This device allows one to practice dribbling a basketball without having to chase after it.

A most interesting invention was reported by a third student, Linda Wagner. This is the "self-injector," shown in Fig. 7.22, which is used for giving oneself allergy shots just under the skin. The rubber half sphere is first squeezed and placed on the skin, creating a vacuum and drawing the skin up. The shot can then be administered without having to observe the needle penetrating the skin.

SPANNING THE CATEGORIES

I next turned to an additional challenge—to see if a single preinventive form could span all eight of the object categories. That is, I wanted to see whether the same preinventive form could be interpreted as eight different types of inventions. Previous studies have shown, for example, that it is often possible to interpret a single perceptually ambiguous form as recognizable objects belonging to many different object categories (e.g., Shepard & Cermak, 1973). I wondered if this would also be possible using preinventive forms.

I began by generating six preinventive forms after being given new sets of randomly chosen parts, and then selected one of these forms for the interpretations. The particular form I used is shown in Fig. 7.23. I then had the computer generate the names of the eight object categories in random order, and I attempted to interpret my preinventive form according to each of the categories.

The resulting inventions are shown in Fig. 7.24. First, for the category "furniture," I saw the preinventive form as a "lawn lounger," which can be used as an outdoor lawn chair. The half sphere is made of soft material, and the hook provides support to the ground.

For the category "personal items," my invention was the "global earrings." Each earring depicts a different half of the world, enabling the wearer to be at the center of it.

For the category "scientific instruments," my invention was the "water weigher." You fill the half sphere with water, then attach an object to be weighed to the hook. If the object exceeds a certain weight, it will tip the bowl and spill the water.

For the category "appliances," my invention was the "portable agitator." One places clothes in the tub, and then turns the crank back and forth to clean and agitate the clothes. The hook allows the clothes to be hung in the sun to dry.

For the category "transportation," my invention was the "water sled." This is

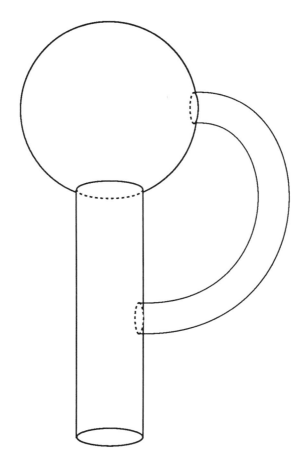

FIG. 7.20. The "adjustable playground," constructed using the CYLINDER, SPHERE, and TUBE. Children climb up into the transparent dome and slide down the tube, which can be repositioned in various ways.

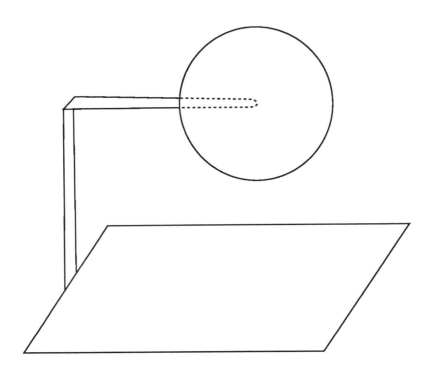

FIG. 7.21.   The "basketball dribbler," constructed using the FLAT SQUARE, BRACKET, and SPHERE. The device allows one to practice dribbling without having to chase after the ball.

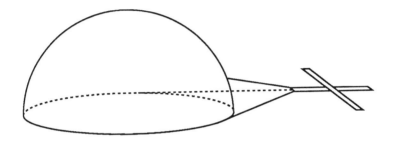

FIG. 7.22. The "self-injector," constructed using the CONE, HALF SPHERE, and CROSS. Used for giving oneself allergy shots just under the skin. The rubber half sphere is squeezed and then placed on the skin, drawing the skin up; the shot is then administered without having to observe it.

FIG. 7.23. Preinventive form used by the author in attempting to span each of the eight object categories, constructed using the BRACKET, HOOK, and HALF SPHERE.

FIG. 7.24. Interpretations of the preinventive form shown in Figure 7.23, spanning the eight object categories as follows: "lawn lounger" (furniture), "global earrings" (personal items), "water weigher" (scientific instruments), "portable agitator" (appliances), "water sled" (transportation), "rotating masher" (tools & utensils), "ring spinner" (toys & games), and "slasher basher" (weapons).

a floating sled that you can use to travel down rapids, for example. You steer it by shifting your weight while turning the "handlebar," like a bicycle.

For the category "tools and utensils," my invention was the "rotating masher." This is used to mash and grind things in a bowl. You hold the stem with one hand and turn the handle with the other; it mixes and grinds at the same time.

For the category "toys and games," my invention was the "ring spinner." The device rotates like a top, and the object of the game is to toss rings onto the hook before it stops rotating.

Finally, for the category "weapons," my invention was the "slasher basher." The weapon is held by the central stem, and one uses it to slash or bash while protecting one's hand. This, however, is one invention I would not care to own.

In doing this task, the only difficulty I encountered was in coming up with the *second* interpretation. Once I had done so, it was easy to discover other interpretations. My students also noted this; that when the preinventive form was interpreted for the first time, it was hard to see it as something else—even though the initial interpretation was arbitrary. Perhaps a kind of psychological "cohesiveness" is created once a preinventive form is interpreted, which inhibits one from using the same preinventive form again with the same fluidity. As soon as another interpretation is found, however, such inhibitions may no longer exist.

SUMMARY AND IMPLICATIONS

These informal demonstrations suggest that the techniques may have enormous practical value when used without the extreme time constraints that were employed in the experiments of the previous chapters. Under these more favorable conditions, it may be possible to generate a new invention on virtually every attempt. Further, it is evident that people can easily be taught to use these techniques for a variety of inventive purposes. I will consider specific recommendations for their general use in Chapter 9.

Also, I should comment briefly on the apparent spontaneity with which many of these inventions were discovered. Few of these inventions arose in what might be considered great "leaps" of insight, where the pathway to the invention was totally obscure. On the contrary, most of the inventions followed deliberate strategies of exploration. This is not to say, however, that the inventions themselves were derived in a calculated way. Indeed, the final discovery of the inventions was nearly always surprising and completely unexpected. Exploring the preinventive forms in sensible ways may simply increase the likelihood that spontaneous, creative discoveries can be made.

Chapter
8

Creative Concepts

The two previous chapters have demonstrated that preinventive forms can lead to the discovery of creative inventions for practical objects and devices. The experiments I report in the present chapter extend the idea of using preinventive forms to the discovery of creative concepts and principles. In particular, these next experiments address the issue of whether these same methods can be used to make creative discoveries in scientific and artistic fields, such as physics, medicine, psychology, music, and literature. This will bring us closer to what seems to be happening in the "Kekulé" phenomenon, where a mental image is seen to "represent" a new conceptual or theoretical insight.

Note that many of the creative object inventions reported in the preceding chapters can also be considered "conceptual" discoveries, in that the preinventive forms represented the key concept underlying the invention, which would then need some further refinement to actually work. That is, the preinventive forms often inspired the essential idea behind the invention, but did not necessarily depict it in its final, polished form.

In view of the previous successes that subjects had in interpreting their preinventive forms, I wanted to see how far the methods could be "pushed" in the direction of conceptual discovery. Could preinventive forms also serve as "visual metaphors" for purely conceptual insights? And if so, how successfully could these methods be applied by undergraduate students having no prior training or preparation?

A PARADIGM FOR CONCEPTUAL DISCOVERY
(EXPERIMENTS 8–9)

These experiments were similar in overall structure to Experiment 6, the original "preinventive form" experiment (see Chapter 6), except that *subject* categories were now used in place of *object* categories, and the goal of the task was to interpret the preinventive forms as representing a new idea or theory that pertained to those categories, as opposed to a specific kind of invention. In other words, the preinventive forms were now to be considered as symbolic depictions of abstract concepts, rather than literal depictions of concrete objects.

I originally came up with the idea for doing these experiments while thinking about the preinventive form shown in Fig. 8.1. Several days before, I had gone through a series of allergy tests, and was surprised to learn that all of the tests were negative, since I knew that I had had allergic reactions to at least some of the foods and pollens for which I was tested. This was on the back of my mind as I pondered the preinventive form. Suddenly, I had the insight that maybe I was allergic to certain *interactions* among allergens; the preinventive form suggesting that two different pollens had combined to create a reaction. I realized that this could explain the negative results of my tests, as each of the allergens had been considered individually. This led me to the concept of "interacting allergies," and suggested the idea for extending the previous methods.

Overall, I expected that this version of the task should be much harder, as indeed it was. Although undergraduate students would have had some experience with all of the concrete object categories used in the previous experiments, they would not necessarily have sufficient background experience with categories representing particular fields of study. For instance, a person might be knowledgeable in music or literature, but not in physics or biology. I therefore decided to conduct two versions of the experiment, varying whether or not the subjects were free to choose their own subject category after having constructed their preinventive forms.

My initial expectation was that the subjects would do much better when they could choose which category to use when interpreting their forms. This seemed reasonable, as they could then apply their expertise, compared to when they were merely given an arbitrarily chosen subject category. And this expectation was completely wrong, for reasons that become obvious only in retrospect.

EXPERIMENTAL PROCEDURES

The procedure for Experiment 8 will be described first. As in the previous experiments on creative invention, 60 subjects were tested using six trials per subject, the parts were randomly selected for each trial, and naive experimenters conducted the study. The experiment began exactly as Experiment 6, with subjects

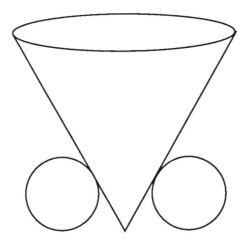

FIG. 8.1. The concept of "interacting allergies," represented using the SPHERE, SPHERE, and CONE. The idea is that certain substances may cause allergic reactions when they occur together, where neither one alone would cause a reaction.

receiving instructions for generating preinventive forms at the beginning of each trial, again being told that the forms should correspond to an object that is interesting and potentially useful in a general sense, rather than corresponding to a specific, concrete object. As before, they were given 1 minute to generate each of the preinventive forms in imagination, while keeping their eyes closed, and were then asked to draw the forms. The experimenter then described the eight subject categories that would be used.

These categories are shown in Table 8.1. The subjects were told that one of the categories would be randomly chosen on each trial, and would be named after they had finished drawing their forms. They would then be asked to interpret the object as representing a new idea or concept belonging to that category. The particular categories were selected to provide a broad range of different fields of study.

The subjects were then given several examples of the kinds of conceptual interpretations that might be appropriate for each category. For example, they were told that for the category "architecture," they might interpret the object as representing a new concept in building design. For the category "physics and astronomy," their object might represent a new model of the atom, or how the universe was formed. For the category "biology," their object might represent a new concept in animal survival, or a new possibility in evolutionary theory. For the category "medicine," their object might represent a new theory for how a virus might invade a cell, or a new way of curing a disease. For the category "psychology," their object might represent a new theory of personality or how the mind works. For the category "literature," their object might represent a new kind of writing style, or a new strategy for writing a novel. For the category "music," their object might represent a new idea for composing a song, or a new way that instruments might be combined. For the category "political science," their object might represent a new form of government or political theory.

These detailed instructions were given so that the subjects would understand that the interpretations could be very abstract. They were told, specifically, that

TABLE 8.1
Allowable Subject Categories Used in Experiments
on Creative Concepts

Category	*Examples*
1. ARCHITECTURE	Concepts in Building Design, etc.
2. PHYSICS AND ASTRONOMY	Models of the Atom, Universe, etc.
3. BIOLOGY	Methods of Animal Survival, etc.
4. MEDICINE	Mechanisms of Infection, etc.
5. PSYCHOLOGY	Theories of Personality, etc.
6. LITERATURE	Writing Styles, Techniques, etc.
7. MUSIC	Composition, Instrumentation, etc.
8. POLITICAL SCIENCE	Forms of Government, etc.

the objects did not have to actually have to look like something specific, but could simply suggest the concept or idea. In addition, they were shown actual examples, from pilot studies, of six preinventive forms and conceptual interpretations that could be given to them, to make sure that they understood that the preinventive forms were not to be interpreted merely as concrete objects.

As in Experiment 6, the subjects were given 1 minute to interpret their objects after the category name was given. They were then to name the subject category and to describe their concepts on the response sheets.

The concepts were rated by judges in the same way as before, except that the dimension of "Practicality" was replaced by "Sensibility," which referred to how sensible the concept was. This was done because a concept may make a great deal of sense, but not necessarily be "practical." To be classified as a "Sensible Concept," the concept had to receive a combined rating of at least "9" on the Sensibility dimension, and to be classified as a "Creative Concept," it had to be a sensible concept that received a combined rating of at least "8" on the Originality dimension. As with the ratings for creative inventions, this convention was conservative, in that it excluded those ideas that did not appear sensible, regardless of how creative they might be.

In Experiment 9, a similar procedure was followed using a different group of 60 subjects, except that the subjects were now permitted to choose their own subject category from the list of those provided in Table 8.1 when they began to interpret their preinventive forms. As previously mentioned, this would seem to be an easier condition for the subjects, as they could then select whichever category might best conform to their own areas of expertise.

RESULTS OF THE EXPERIMENTS

First, as expected, the conceptual interpretation task was harder than the previous tasks, where the subjects had interpreted their forms as specific, concrete inventions. As shown in Table 8.2, subjects in Experiments 8 and 9 interpreted their preinventive forms as sensible concepts on 15.0% of the trials, and as creative concepts on 5.7% of the trials. By comparison, subjects in Experiment 6 had come up with practical and creative inventions on 33.3% and 18.1% of the trials, respectively. Even so, across the two experiments, there were a total of 41 unique concepts that were classified as "creative," indicating that the methods can be extended with at least some success to the domain of conceptual interpretation.

Surprisingly, performance was better when the subjects could *not* choose the conceptual categories. As also shown in Table 8.2, subjects who were given specific categories to use in their conceptual interpretations produced more than twice as many creative concepts, $\chi^2 (1) = 5.48$, $p < .05$, and seven of the nine concepts that were classified as highly creative. Whereas 45.9% of the sensible concepts were classified as creative in Experiment 8, in Experiment 9 this was

TABLE 8.2
Number of Sensible, Creative and Highly Creative Concepts
Reported by Subjects According to Whether The Subject Category
was Chosen or Randomly Specified (Experiments 8–9)

Type of Concept	Condition	
	Subject Category Random	*Subject Category Chosen*
Sensible	61	47
Creative	28	13
Highly Creative	7	2

Note: The above categorizations are based on a total of 720 trials, 360 for each condition. "Creative" concepts were sensible concepts rated as original; "Highly Creative" concepts received the highest possible rating on both sensibility and originality.

true for only 27.7% of the sensible concepts. There were no significant differences between the two experiments in the number of sensible concepts generated, χ^2 (1) = 1.55, $p > .10$.

These results imply that arbitrarily imposing conceptual categories in association with the preinventive forms is better than starting out with the forms and then finding the most suitable categories. How could one explain this counterintuitive result? Inspection of the conceptual interpretations that subjects provided in Experiment 9 suggested a simple answer. Most of these interpretations corresponded to superficial ideas—as if the preinventive forms had suggested to the subjects some initial concept that was already familiar to them. By contrast, when the subjects could not chose the subject category, they had to explore the deeper implications of the preinventive forms, even though they may not have had much knowledge about the subject. Recall that in Chapter 4, subjects were less creative in coming up with inventions when they were allowed to choose the categories or the parts, which tended to result in conventional ideas—compared to when both the parts and categories were arbitrarily specified. This again speaks to the importance of being committed to explore the unexpected possibilities of the preinventive forms.

Accordingly, the results of Experiment 8 cannot be attributed simply to the subjects having associated the forms in novel ways with concepts that were already familiar to them. Indeed, given a greater opportunity to make such associations, as in Experiment 9, the conceptual interpretations were much less creative.

Perhaps not surprisingly, there were striking individual differences in these experiments. Some of the subjects could not come up with a single sensible concept; others could do so with a wonderful sense of inspiration. Overall, in Experiment 8, 33.3% of the subjects were able to come up with at least one creative concept, whereas only 18.3% of the subjects in Experiment 9 were able to do so.

As an aside, I should mention that subjects in Experiment 9 did not tend to choose a particular category more than the others (in case readers might think the subjects were all psychology majors who chose "Psychology" as the category). Rather, the choice of categories seemed motivated more by the initial impressions of the preinventive forms. This was not an effective strategy, however, in that being able to choose the category after generating the forms resulted in fewer creative ideas.

As usual, there were no significant practice effects in either of the experiments (For all χ^2 tests, $p > .10$). As with the creative object inventions, the generation of creative concepts appears to be a fairly spontaneous process.

EXAMPLES OF CREATIVE CONCEPTS

I next present examples of some of the creative concepts that were reported in these experiments. A complete list of the creative concepts is provided in Table 8.3.

In Fig. 8.2, the preinventive form represents the concept of "captured concepts." The idea is that free-floating concepts and thoughts may be "captured" by those that are already well- grounded or part of an existing conceptual structure. It is similar to the notion of a "schema" in research on human memory (e.g., Bartlett, 1932; Bower, Black, & Turner, 1979; Bransford & Johnson, 1972).

The concept of "conceptual distancing" is shown in Fig. 8.3. The idea is that people who think or believe in much the same way often keep a certain distance between them in a relationship. The intuition represented here is that there is something personally threatening about sharing too many of the same concepts.

Figure 8.4 illustrates the concept of "prefission bonding." The idea is that, in order to split atoms, subatomic particles must first be bonded temporarily to them. This bonding would precede the actual fission process.

The architectural concept of "quakeproof support" is presented in Fig. 8.5. The ring-and-pivot support could compensate for moderate structural displacements during earthquakes. This would be particularly useful, for example, in constructing bridges and other elevated structures.

Figure 8.6 illustrates the concept of "social adhesion." As a model for political or social conformity, the idea is that a large social network having a strong support encourages others to join or become attached to it.

The literary concept of "stylistic containment" is presented in Fig. 8.7. The idea is that a writer begins with a very broad subject, then quickly narrows and contains it, concentrating on a particular topic, and finally broadens it again at

TABLE 8.3
List of Concepts Classified as Creative and Highly Creative
(Experiments 8 and 9)

amino barriers	melodic synthesis
* CAPTURED CONCEPTS	metaphorical elaboration
channeled stability	* modular memories
collective culture	musical extraction
combinational simplicity	musical shapes
compositional cone	note hesitation
CONCEPTUAL DISTANCING	* pathways of intelligence
conceptual flow	poetic convergence
conical construction	PREFISSION BONDING
converging melodies	QUAKEPROOF SUPPORT
cooperative infection	* rules of peace
creative blocking	regenerating antibodies
deceptive dryness	site-specific infection
destroyer proteins	* SOCIAL ADHESION
developmental indifference	* STYLISTIC CONTAINMENT
domineering dependence	* TOLERANCE OF ABUSE
expanded melodies	* VIRAL CANCELLATION
heat trapping	virus trap
instrumental balance	votes of truth
literary ascendance	window cones
* literary genesis	

Note: Creative concepts that were also classified as "Highly Creative" are denoted by an asterisk. The creative concepts that are described in the text are capitalized.

the conclusion. This is done while keeping everything contained within the existing structure or theme.

A model representing "tolerance of abuse" is presented in Fig. 8.8. The basic idea is that the human body (depicted by the spring) can tolerate only a certain amount of abuse (depicted by the weighted cylinder) and fully recover. If the "weight" of abuse is too great, the body will not return completely back to normal after being released from the abuse. For example, a toxin may have reversible effects at small doses but irreversible effects at larger doses.

Finally, the concept of "viral cancellation" is represented in Fig. 8.9. The idea is that two viruses attempting to invade the same cell may "cancel" one another, curing or preventing the disease. This would imply that in order to cure one illness, it may be necessary to expose oneself to another illness.

One might question how original these conceptual discoveries truly are, for admittedly, only experts in a field could make such evaluations. For example, it would not be surprising if someone in the field of immunology had already thought of the idea of "interacting allergies" that I introduced at the beginning of the chapter. But this is really beside the point. The key issue, again, is whether these methods can stimulate people to discover ideas for concepts that seem

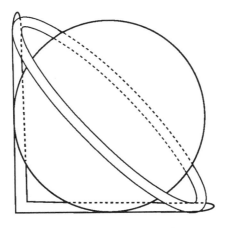

FIG. 8.2. The concept of "captured concepts," represented using the SPHERE, BRACKET, and RING. The idea is that free-floating concepts and thoughts may be "captured" by those that are already well-grounded or part of an existing conceptual structure.

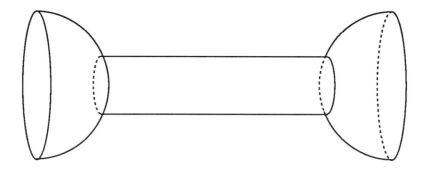

FIG. 8.3. The concept of "conceptual distancing," represented using the CYLINDER, HALF SPHERE, and HALF SPHERE. The idea is that people who think or believe in much the same way often keep a certain distance between them in a relationship.

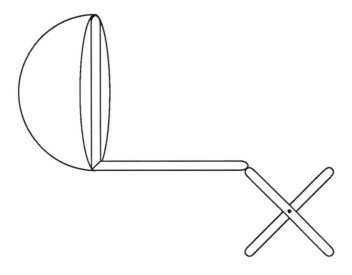

FIG. 8.4. The concept of "prefission bonding," represented using the CROSS, HALF SPHERE, and BRACKET. The idea is that in order to split atoms, subatomic particles must be temporarily bonded to them.

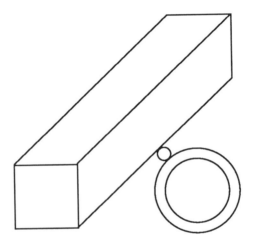

FIG. 8.5. The concept of "quakeproof support," represented using the RECTANGULAR BLOCK, SPHERE, and RING. The idea is that the ring-and-pivot support could compensate for moderate structural displacements during earthquakes; for example, in bridges and other elevated structures.

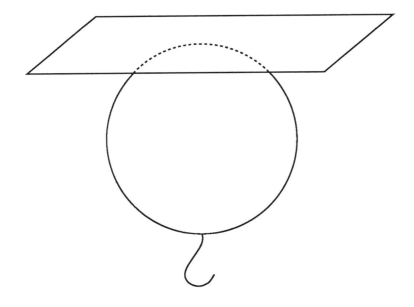

FIG. 8.6. The concept of "social adhesion," represented using the HOOK, SPHERE, and FLAT SQUARE. The idea is that a large social network having a strong support encourages others to join or become attached to it.

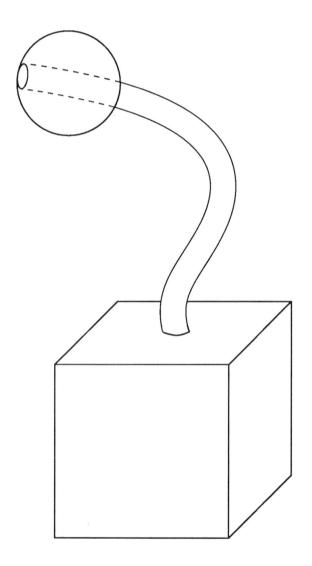

FIG. 8.7. The concept of "stylistic containment," represented using the CUBE, TUBE, and SPHERE. The idea is that a writer begins with a very broad subject, then quickly narrows and contains it, concentrating on a particular topic, and finally broadens it again at the conclusion.

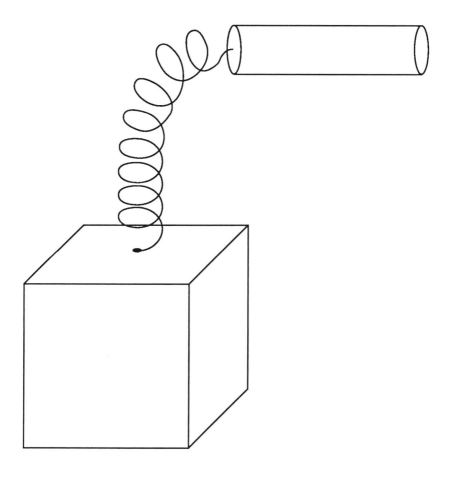

FIG. 8.8.   The concept of "tolerance of abuse," represented using the CUBE, WIRE, and CYLINDER. The idea is that the human body can tolerate only a certain amount of abuse and fully recover; if the "weight" of abuse is too great, the body will not return completely back to normal after being released from the abuse.

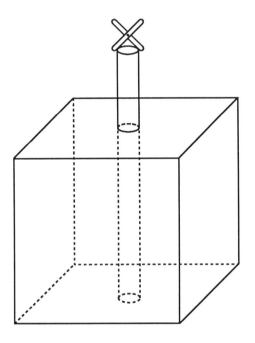

FIG. 8.9. The concept of "viral cancellation," represented using the TUBE, CROSS, and CUBE. The idea is that two viruses attempting to invade a cell may "cancel" one another, curing or preventing the disease.

potentially important to them, and which lead them to new insights, not whether someone else might have previously thought of the same concepts. The exciting thing about these methods, I think, is that they give people an opportunity to make conceptual discoveries that they might not have made otherwise. Whether the ideas are original in an absolute sense is actually quite irrelevant for purposes of these investigations.

READER PARTICIPATION: CREATIVE CONCEPTS

I would now like to give readers the same opportunity to make their own conceptual discoveries, using the technique of interpreting their preinventive forms. In Table 8.4, sets of parts are provided for generating the preinventive forms. As before, visualize and record each of the forms before going on to the next step. Now, using the subject categories listed in Table 8.5, try to interpret your preinventive forms as new ideas or concepts within those categories. I would be interested in knowing if any of these example trials led you to new creative insights.

PERSONAL CONCEPTUAL DISCOVERIES

I would also like to present several of my own conceptual discoveries using the methods developed in Experiment 8. Again, I cannot guarantee that these ideas are entirely original within these particular fields of study, only that I myself have never thought of any of them before.

TABLE 8.4
Examples of Sets of Parts Used in Experiments on Generating
Creative Concepts

1.	HALF SPHERE WIRE CROSS	6.	RECTANGULAR BLOCK CONE BRACKET
2.	BRACKET CROSS CROSS	7.	CONE BRACKET FLAT SQUARE
3.	FLAT SQUARE WIRE WIRE	8.	CYLINDER WHEELS WIRE
4.	CUBE WHEELS CONE	9.	SPHERE CONE SPHERE
5.	SPHERE BRACKET CYLINDER	10.	FLAT SQUARE CUBE HALF SPHERE

Note: These sets of parts are to be used in conjunction with the subject categories provided in Table 8.5, but only *after* the preinventive forms are generated.

TABLE 8.5
Examples of Subject Categories That Were Randomly Paired With
Sets of Parts After the Preinventive Forms Were Generated

1.	PHYSICS AND ASTRONOMY	6.	LITERATURE
2.	MUSIC	7.	MUSIC
3.	ARCHITECTURE	8.	PSYCHOLOGY
4.	PSYCHOLOGY	9.	BIOLOGY
5.	PHYSICS AND ASTRONOMY	10.	MEDICINE

Note: These categories are to be used with the corresponding sets of parts listed in Table 8.4.

Using informal procedures similar to those described in Chapter 7, I began by generating preinventive forms for 24 sets of parts, allowing myself 1 minute per form. I then attempted to interpret each of the forms according to particular subject categories that were randomly selected by a computer. As in Experiment 8, I did not know what the category would be until after I had completed my preinventive forms. I allowed myself a maximum time of 15 minutes to interpret the forms.

As with the experimental subjects, I, too, found this task somewhat harder than the previous tasks. On 2 of the 24 trials, for example, I failed to come up with a sensible concept for the designated category. Nevertheless, I was able to use this method to make conceptual discoveries most of the time. And, as with my discoveries of inventions described in the previous chapter, the suddenness with which many of these insights came was particularly striking.

In Fig. 8.10, I present the architectural concept of "cones of light." The idea is that an array of lights pointing diagonally downward from inside a suspended cone can create the impression of a luminous "cone" of light, which can be used, for example, to adorn the tops of buildings. (Here I imagined looking at the form and mentally "seeing" the cones of light descending from it.)

Another architectural concept, that of "dynamic facades," is presented in Fig. 8.11. The idea is that a building can be enhanced by displaying large, rotating disks of art on opposite sides. These rotating disks can add a dynamic quality to a city's skyline. (Initially, I imagined seeing this as a large downtown building, with mysterious turning disks. When I imagined looking at the disks from the side, I could mentally "see" them as artforms.)

The concept of "embedded cognitions" is presented in Fig. 8.12. The idea is that by moving cognitive processes farther apart (represented by the rotating tube and the ring), you dissociate them, whereas by bringing them together, one becomes embedded in the other. (I imagined the tube and the ring spinning around, and then mentally "saw" the implications of their interactions as cognitive processes.)

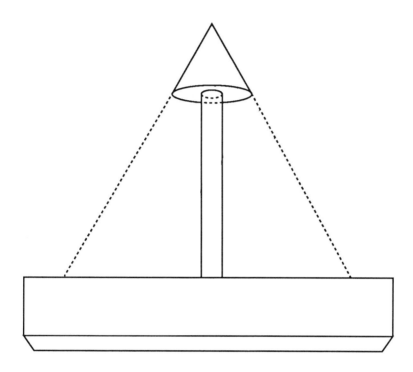

FIG. 8.10.   The concept of "cones of light," represented using the CONE, CYLINDER, and RECTANGULAR BLOCK. The idea is that an array of lights pointing diagonally downward from inside a suspended cone can create the illusion of a luminous "cone" of light.

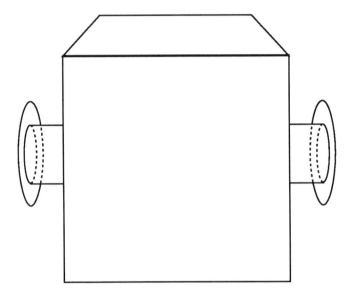

FIG. 8.11.   The concept of "dynamic facades," represented using the WHEELS, CUBE, and CYLINDER. The idea is that a building can be enhanced by displaying large, rotating disks of art on opposite sides.

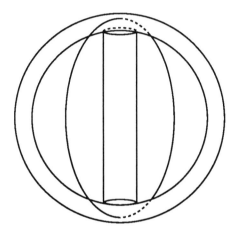

FIG. 8.12.   The concept of "embedded cognitions," represented using the TUBE, RING, and CYLINDER. The idea is that by moving cognitive processes farther apart, you dissociate them, whereas by bringing them together, one becomes embedded in the other.

A literary concept, "frames of synthesis," is presented in Fig. 8.13. As two imaginary frames of mind are created, the writer moves freely between them, eventually achieving a new synthesis. (I imagined a writer "moving" from one sphere to the other as the spheres enlarged, making more and more connections between them.)

I also present an example of a creative concept that one of my students, Donna McKeown, discovered using the same methods. She interpreted the preinventive form shown in Fig. 8.14 as representing the concept of "retractable receptors." The idea is that receptors for hormones or chemical messages might have a "retractable" property, in that they could withdraw their receptive capacity under certain conditions.

SUMMARY

This final set of experiments shows that the method of interpreting preinventive forms can be extended to the domain of conceptual discovery. These techniques evidently work best when people cannot chose the subject category to fit the preinventive form, but must use a particular, designated category. Overall, subjects were less successful in coming up with creative concepts compared to the previous experiments, where they could interpret their preinventive forms as concrete object inventions. Nevertheless, the results of Experiment 8 suggest that preinventive forms can be interpreted as symbolic representations of novel concepts to at least some extent.

THEORETICAL IMPLICATIONS

Consider, again, the Kekulé phenomenon: A scientist involved in a particular field of study, concerned with a specific class of problems, who suddenly has an image of a preinventive form, and sees how the form can provide the necessary insight to solve one of the problems within that domain. Contrast this situation with that in which a person attempts to discover virtually any concept which might fit a preinventive form. In the latter case, there is simply too much flexibility in the interpretation. One does not have to interpret the form very deeply at all, and is thereby denied the opportunity of having the genuinely surprising, creative insights that great scientists and artists so frequently report. In this sense, subjects in Experiment 9 were *misusing* their preinventive forms.

The notion, here, is that one needs to be committed to searching for new ideas within a specific conceptual domain. It can't be completely open-ended; you get conceptually "snowblinded"—as with the beginning writer who has complete freedom to write on any topic, and gets writer's block. Restricting the conceptual domain makes you explore a preinventive form in nontrivial ways. Hence, prein-

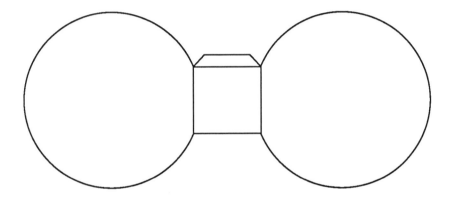

FIG. 8.13.   The concept of "frames of synthesis," represented using the SPHERE, CUBE, and SPHERE. The idea is that as two imaginary frames of mind are created, the writer moves freely between them, eventually achieving a new synthesis.

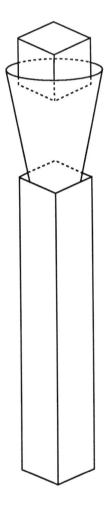

FIG. 8.14. The concept of "retractable receptors," represented using the RECTAN-GULAR BLOCK, CONE, and CUBE. The idea is that receptors for hormones or chemical messages might have a "retractable" property, in that they could withdraw their receptive capacity under certain conditions.

ventive forms are probably most helpful when one is already thinking about a particular topic or class of problems.

Yet, there are surely limits to how much you would want to restrict the conceptual interpretations. For example, if you specified, instead of a concept in "physics," the requirement that the preinventive form had to represent "a new model of the atom," you would probably find that that one particular form would not represent any reasonable model. Recall that in Experiment 4, where subjects were restricted in the types of objects they could invent, they came up with far fewer inventions, compared to subjects who could work within an entire object category. Thus, if one is concerned about coming up with a specific invention, or solving a specific problem, it might be better to generate many preinventive forms for that purpose, and then allow enough time to explore the less obvious interpretive possibilities.

The reader may note an apparent contradiction between the poor performance of subjects in Experiment 9, and the expectation that people ought to generate more creative ideas in their own fields of specialization. Wouldn't experts in a field be "choosing" the subject categories when attempting to use these methods? And wasn't it shown that this is precisely the situation that promotes superficial interpretations of the preinventive forms?

It is important, I think, to distinguish between committing yourself to a particular category *before* you know what the preinventive form will be, and doing so only afterwards. In the former case, we have the Kekulé phenomenon: a scientist already committed to solving problems within a conceptual domain, who recognizes how the imagined structures could apply to those problems. In the latter case, we have the conditions of Experiment 9, where superficial interpretations of the forms arise because one is *not* committed, in advance, to trying to make discoveries within a particular conceptual domain. Rather, one simply decides on the category after knowing what the preinventive forms look like.

The idea that preinventive forms can give rise to insights about general problems that people might be concerned about is considered at length in the final chapter.

Chapter

9

Creative Implications

REVIEW OF EXPERIMENTAL FINDINGS

The experiments reported in this book lead to the following general conclusions: People are capable of making visual discoveries using mental imagery, and these discoveries are not merely the result of sophisticated guessing, experimenter bias, or skilled anticipation. To make creative discoveries in imagery, it seems best to imagine combining basic parts or components in an intuitive, exploratory way, and then mentally "seeing" if an interesting shape or form emerges. To discover ideas for creative inventions, it is better, first of all, to restrict the range of object categories to be considered and the particular parts to be used. Second, it is better to commit oneself to imagining preinventive forms of general interest and potential usefulness, and to then interpret the forms according to particular object categories, than to use the object categories to motivate the forms. Third, it is better to use preinventive forms that one generates oneself, rather than those provided by others, implying that there is more to the act of discovering creative inventions than simply coming up with creative interpretations. Finally, in extending these methods to the discovery of creative concepts, it is better to consider how the preinventive forms might relate to a particular field of study, than to try to relate the forms to any field of study whatsoever.

Additional findings of these experiments suggest that the creative discoveries that occur in imagery are similar to those that occur when the parts can actually be manipulated and combined, and that the discoveries are often "spontaneous," in that they occur unexpectedly, do not increase with practice, and are not affected by having seen examples of other mental constructions using the same parts.

Taken together, these findings imply that creative discoveries are inspired by the emergent properties of the preinventive forms themselves.

A RECONCEPTUALIZATION OF CREATIVITY

In view of these findings, I would like to propose some new ways of thinking about creative imagery in particular, and creativity in general. These considerations follow from the nature and function of preinventive forms.

First, creativity should be considered as the pathway, not the solution. By this I mean that creativity should not be thought of in terms of the specific products of the creative act, but rather, as the way one engages in creative exploration. The same preinventive forms, for example, can lead one to many different kinds of creative insights and discoveries; they need not be focused on a particular problem or type of invention. The essence of creative invention is not the final product, but how we arrive there.

In this sense, creativity is using the things we create, not creating the things we use. This, I believe, is why preinventive forms often lead to inventions and insights that seem so elegant and resourceful in retrospect. The forms can be interpreted in a more natural way when they are not manufactured to fit a particular need or problem. Indeed, there is often something unnatural and unsatisfying about the "makeshift" kinds of inventions or solutions that serve an immediate purpose.

This implies that creative insights are largely accidental events. When interpreting preinventive forms, for example, one often makes discoveries that were not mandated by the requirements of the task. Rather, the inventions often provide solutions to problems that were not being considered, or do not yet exist. In other words, the "tasking" of an idea should not come first if you want the idea to be creative. You fit the task to the creation, not the other way around.

This leads me to believe that creative problem solving is largely a matter of coincidence, and not the result of an intelligent unconscious. A popular explanation for creative scientific insights, such as that of Kekulé, is that unconscious mental processes solve the problem and then "alert" the conscious mind by way of image representations (e.g., Weisberg, 1986). It makes more sense, however, to think that Kekulé's image was simply a useful preinventive form, which could have been interpreted in many other meaningful, creative ways, had other problems been on his mind.

I therefore reject the notion that unconscious mental processes are responsible for creative solutions or insights. The unconscious may be more aesthetic, causing us to think about interesting forms and structures, but how could it be more *intelligent?* Kekulé's insight came about because the right preinventive form appeared in his mind at the right time. His image representing the structure of a benzene molecule might have been interpreted as an architectural concept or the design for a new style of furniture, had these been his primary concerns. No doubt other preinventive forms had also entered his mind, but were then forgotten, because they didn't happen to make contact with the benzene problem.

Thus, whereas unconscious mental processes may guide the aesthetic qualities of a preinventive form, and may lead us to think that there is something potentially important about the form, they do not determine the recognition and interpretation of the form, and hence, do not create the inventions or solutions. Again, true creativity is using the things we create.

What about evidence for "incubation," where a person discovers the solution to a problem after not having thought about it for a period of time? (e.g., see Olton, 1979; Smith & Blankenship, 1989). Is this because unconscious mental processes have gone to work on the solution? I think not. In light of the previous considerations, incubation may work simply because it would help one to move away from preconceived notions when interpreting preinventive forms. As the experiments in this book have shown, creative discoveries are more likely when one cannot simply associate the preinventive forms with familiar ideas, but must explore the deeper implications of the forms.

This approach to creative thinking and discovery is more like artistic creation that finds its purpose, rather than creation that satisfies a purpose. Consider an artist, for example, who begins by combining visual forms in an intuitive way, and then realizes what compositions might follow from those forms. Or, the composer who first writes down the melodies that come into his head and then realizes where the melodies belong. This is similar to how one might discover inventions or concepts that belong to a preinventive form. Creativity, so conceived, is discovering the pathway that allows one's intuitions to mature.

PREINVENTIVE FORMS AND PROBLEM SOLVING

How do preinventive forms function in the whole scheme of creative problem solving? I think they would serve mainly as catalysts, leading one to discover the kinds of solutions that might bear on a particular class of problems. The basic idea is that the same preinventive form could mediate between many different problems and solutions that have an underlying structure in common. This is why it is better not to focus in on too narrow a problem when trying to interpret the preinventive forms.

As preinventive forms lead one to discover new concepts or insights, what was regarded as the original problem or concern might change. That is, as possible solutions come forth, the problems themselves might shift, as one comes to recognize new solution possibilities. Thus, the "tasking" of the situation may get redefined in the very act of creative problem solving.

This approach can be contrasted with other approaches typically used in problem solving. For example, in what is called "means-end" analysis, one first defines the characteristics of the desired solution and then explores ways that bring one progressively closer to that solution (e.g., Hayes, 1981; Newell & Simon, 1972). I am advocating something very much the opposite—one searches for creative insights for potential solutions to problems without specifying what the precise nature of those solutions must be.

This approach is also distinct from that of "working backwards," in which one begins with a solution and then seeks to discover how the solution maps onto the problem (e.g., Wickelgren, 1974). One does not start with a well-defined solution; one starts with preinventive forms that suggest possible solutions. In this sense, the approach is more like working "inwards," in that you seek to discover what the interesting solutions might be, to problems you may not have even thought about.

At the same time, however, you need to have some constraints on the kinds of solutions you are willing to consider. As the experiments on creative concepts showed, for instance, it is more difficult to discover conceptual insights when a preinventive form can be interpreted as any concept whatsoever. Restricting the interpretation to a particular conceptual category or problem domain would therefore be an important aspect of using preinventive forms for solving problems. You don't restrict the range of interpretations too narrowly, nor do you allow them to vary without restriction.

Of course, one *could* try to use preinventive forms to search for narrowly defined solutions to a problem, but this would take much more time and commitment. This is why it is better to consider general types of solution possibilities. It is natural to come up with creative solutions to something that wasn't part of the original problem. This is the essence of creative search and exploration; if you are too narrowly focused, you run the risk of throwing away the most important creative insights.

Finally, there is the matter of patience in using these methods to discover creative solutions. If a preinventive form seems intriguing, or potentially meaningful, but its exact meaning is not immediately apparent, be patient and explore the preinventive form in other ways. Allow it to make contact with possible insights that you did not expect. Again, remember that the problems may change with the solutions.

IMPLICATIONS FOR THEORIES OF PERCEPTION AND COGNITION

Some may ask why I have not attempted to develop a formal model of how preinventive forms are used in creative insight and discovery. As I have argued in a previous book (Finke, 1989), I believe the concern with developing formal, computational models of psychological processes has led us to overlook some of the important underlying principles. In that book, I suggested that perhaps the best approach for making scientific discoveries was that of "intuitive spreading," in which one begins by seeking out interesting findings and then allows one's intuitions to spread, making contact with other meaningful findings and concepts, with the hope that the underlying principles will "emerge" naturally, as opposed to trying to "demystify" one's intuitions using computational models (e.g., Kosslyn, 1980).

The idea of using preinventive forms to discover inventions and concepts is very much in the same spirit. The intuitively guided conception and exploration of preinventive forms allows one to make new discoveries in a humanly natural way. Whether it might be possible to simulate such discoveries on a computer may be an interesting question for some, but it should not be the foundation for a theory of human creativity. Indeed, I doubt if one could ever construct preinventive forms as effectively, by allowing computers to arrange the parts, without an intuitive sense for the potential interest, value, or inventive possibilities of the forms.

One might criticize my saying little more about the nature of preinventive forms other than they should be "intuitively interesting," "potentially useful," and "personally relevant." But this is precisely the point! As soon as you begin to formalize the preinventive forms, specifying how they should be constructed, you disengage the creative process. This is why I have little interest in examining the specific cognitive operations that might underlie the generation of the preinventive forms.

The concept of exploring preinventive forms is related to the idea, proposed by James Gibson, that perception consists largely of discovering the "affordances" of objects and other features of the environment (J. J. Gibson, 1979). Affordances refer to the potential uses of things; for example, the idea that a hammer affords pounding or that a chair affords sitting. These affordances are considered by Gibson to be directly perceived as one actively explores the environment.

In this sense, I believe that preinventive forms "afford" inventions and new conceptual discoveries. Like the way one perceives the affordances of physical objects, the inventive affordances of preinventive forms are discovered by mentally exploring how the forms might be used. As described in Chapter 7, this might consist of imagining that one is manipulating the forms in various ways. The image discoveries which then "emerge" resemble the way perceptual discoveries can follow the active exploration and manipulation of physical objects (e.g., E. J. Gibson, 1969; J. J. Gibson, 1966).

Perhaps the most important implication of these findings for perceptual and cognitive theories is that they provide striking demonstrations of the essential spatial character of human cognition. Shepard (1978, 1981, 1984), for example, has proposed that much of human thought—particularly, creative thinking—has at its basis the mental representation of spatial structures and their relations. The use of preinventive forms in discovering new inventions and concepts is perhaps the best example of this. I believe the conception of these forms, the recognition of their potential applications, and the discovery of their conceptual interpretations are all part of the inherent, spatial capacities of the human brain. Perhaps, this is part of what makes exploring the preinventive forms so exciting.

ECOLOGICAL SIGNIFICANCE OF THE RESEARCH

The present approach is also in the spirit of efforts to make research on perception and cognition ecologically relevant (e.g., J. J. Gibson, 1979; Neisser, 1976; Shepard, 1984). As opposed to investigating creative thinking in the context of arbitrary or contrived problems and their solutions, the present approach allows people the opportunity to make discoveries which can have direct applications in the real environment. This is one of the reasons, in fact, why readers would truly benefit from learning to use the creative invention techniques that have been presented in this book. I will elaborate next on the possibilities for how these techniques can be used in everyday life.

PRACTICAL IMPLICATIONS IN EVERYDAY LIFE

I would claim, first of all, that most people can benefit from these techniques and be inspired by them. The experiments in Chapter 6, for example, showed that the majority of experimental subjects could use their own preinventive forms to come up with at least one creative invention under fairly severe time restrictions. Moreover, the informal investigations considered in Chapter 7 suggest that it might be possible to come up with a creative invention for every preinventive form that one generates, given sufficient time to interpret the form. Hence, I believe that these methods would have considerable practical value in everyday life applications.

The absence of practice effects in these experiments suggests, furthermore, that the image discoveries are mostly spontaneous. Hence, the successful use of these methods does not require lengthy training procedures. Rather, it is more important to know the best way to go about trying to interpret one's preinventive forms. To this end, I offer some specific suggestions.

First, I would recommend generating preinventive forms that strike you as intuitively appealing, and then recording your preinventive forms in a notebook, for later contemplation and interpretation. Although I believe that the more interesting and intriguing preinventive forms are hard to forget—and indeed, may even impose themselves periodically on one's everyday mentation—it is probably better to record the forms, so that none are disregarded prematurely.

It may be, for example, that what really distinguishes creative from noncreative people is that noncreative people may simply not pursue the possibilities of their creative images. They can generate preinventive forms, but they do not explore them. Here the important notion is that preinventive forms should not be dismissed simply because they do not make immediate sense—for in fact, they may hold the key to new insights, which might be revealed only after you explore the preinventive form for a sufficient length of time.

Next, I think it is essential that you *believe* in your creativity, realizing that everyone is capable of discovering unexpected things in their images. This again speaks to the importance of committing yourself to explore the possibilities of your own preinventive forms. You must believe that a solution or insight will eventually come, though not always the particular one you might have expected. This is where perseverance comes into play.

Finally, as I have said earlier, one should not try to restrict too narrowly the way the preinventive forms can be interpreted, nor should one allow the interpretations to be completely unconstrained. Rather, direct your interpretations to particular classes of objects or conceptual domains of interest. This requires the willingness to explore the preinventive forms in nontrivial ways.

I am therefore recommending three things one could do to promote creative thinking and discovery: (a) generate preinventive forms freely and intuitively, without discarding those that do not lead to new insights right away, (b) explore the possibilities of the preinventive forms patiently and without preconceptions, believing that new discoveries will be found, and (c) concentrate on restricting your interpretations to general classes of objects or concepts, rather than particular types of inventions or problems.

PRACTICAL IMPLICATIONS FOR EXPERTS

If these techniques can be used so successfully with untrained subjects in psychology experiments, consider what experts in a particular field might be able to do—that is, those who could obviously recognize the "deeper" implications of the preinventive forms. A physicist, for example, might be able to interpret a preinventive form as a new concept in particle physics or electrodynamics. An architect might discover a new concept for designing a museum. A doctor might discover a new way to cure an infection. And not to mention the obvious applications of these methods for professional inventors, designers, and engineers.

Businesses could also benefit from using these methods. This would be especially true, for example, where one was interested in coming up with an entirely new concept for a product. Indeed, I suspect that many of the inventions reported in this book could be marketed quite easily. This applies not only to the highly creative inventions that were featured in the illustrations, but also to the hundreds of other inventions that people had discovered in these experiments, which I have listed in the tables.

FURTHER ISSUES AND DIRECTIONS

In this final section, I would like to consider some additional issues bearing on the nature of preinventive forms, and some possible directions for future research. First, it would be worth exploring whether there are different "classes" of preinventive forms, some of which might be more useful for certain applications than others. For example, are preinventive forms that lead to creative inventions equally suitable for discovering conceptual insights in a particular field of study? Or are there certain types of preinventive forms that are useful only for particular types of applications?

A related consideration is whether "universal" preinventive forms exist in any literal sense. If so, I suspect that they would be tied to aesthetics in art somehow. Perhaps one thing that makes a great work of art so appealing is that the forms strike us as personally meaningful and inspiring—stimulating us to think about the possible connections they might have to our own ideas and experiences. In this regard, the appreciation and interpretation of a painting would not be unlike the exploration and interpretation of a preinventive form. A universal preinventive form might be distinguished, therefore, by having a deeper aesthetic appeal.

I can even imagine a new kind of artform in which painting, composing, and even writing styles are deliberately structured to conform to a preinventive form— in much the same way that subjects interpreted their preinventive forms as compositional or literary styles in the experiments of Chapter 8. Artistic creations, so motivated, would engage curiosity and inspire contemplation, resulting in what might come to be regarded as "preinventive art."

Consider, also, the idea that preinventive forms might exist externally in natural structures in the environment. A person looks, for example, at an unusual shape, and "sees" a new idea for a story or invention. I suspect, however, that in such cases it would only be a matter of coincidence if the shapes happened to function as useful preinventive forms. One would be better off exploring the inventive possibilities of preinventive forms that were conceived in imagination.

What is the ideal number of parts that should be used in constructing preinventive forms? In all the experiments reported in this book, three parts were used, mainly because it kept the task simple and did not overload one's capacity for generating and manipulating the imagined parts. Of course, these capacity limitations can be avoided by drawing the preinventive forms instead of imagining them (e.g., see Arnheim, 1969; Torrance, 1974), or by using actual three-dimensional models, which would allow one to consider more complex arrangements of parts. Yet, I wonder if it wouldn't be better to keep the preinventive forms less detailed, to allow room for conceptual flexibility and later refinement. Also, drawing the forms might discourage one from freely manipulating them in imagination.

Another issue to consider in using preinventive forms is when to remain committed to a particular form, and when to discard it in favor of another. We have seen evidence for the broad potential that preinventive forms can have for creative insight and discovery, that they can apply across many conceptual domains. But there must be some limits on the amount of conceptual "baggage" that the same preinventive form can handle. This is an open empirical question.

Finally, I think it would be important to consider the use of preinventive forms in children. In fact, children's drawings seem to represent preinventive forms "in reverse." That is, they depict abstract associations among parts, much as a preinventive form might, but are constructed to represent a specific object or concept. Perhaps, learning to use preinventive forms begins with the exploration of our own attempts at artistic creation.

References

Adams, J. L. (1974). *Conceptual blockbusting*. Stanford, CA: Stanford Alumni Association.

Anderson, J. R. (1978). Arguments concerning representations for mental imagery. *Psychological Review, 85,* 249–277.

Arnheim, R. (1969). *Visual thinking*. Berkeley, CA: University of California Press.

Attneave, F. (1971). Multistability in perception. *Scientific American, 225,* 62–71.

Bartlett, F. C. (1932). *Remembering*. Cambridge, England: Cambridge University Press.

Bethell-Fox, C. E., & Shepard, R. N. (1988). Mental rotation: Effects of stimulus complexity and familiarity. *Journal of Experimental Psychology: Human Perception and Performance, 14,* 12–23.

Biederman, I. (1987). Recognition-by-components: A theory of human image understanding. *Psychological Review, 94,* 115–147.

Bower, G. H., Black, J. B., & Turner, T. J. (1979). Scripts in memory for text. *Cognitive Psychology, 11,* 177–220.

Bransford, J. D., & Johnson, M. K. (1972). Contextual prerequisites for understanding: Some investigations of comprehension and recall. *Journal of Verbal Learning and Verbal Behavior, 11,* 717–721.

Brooks, L. R. (1968). Spatial and verbal components of the act of recall. *Canadian Journal of Psychology, 22,* 349–368.

Bundesen, C., & Larsen, A. (1975). Visual transformation of size. *Journal of Experimental Psychology: Human Perception and Performance, 1,* 214–220.

Chambers, D., & Reisberg, D. (1985). Can mental images be ambiguous? *Journal of Experimental Psychology: Human Perception and Performance, 11,* 317–328.

Cooper, L. A. (1976a). Demonstration of a mental analog of an external rotation. *Perception & Psychophysics, 19,* 296–302.

Cooper, L. A. (1976b). Individual differences in visual comparison processes. *Perception & Psychophysics, 19,* 433–444.

Cooper, L. A., & Podgorny, P. (1976). Mental transformations and visual comparison processes: Effects of complexity and similarity. *Journal of Experimental Psychology: Human Perception and Performance, 2,* 503–514.

Cooper, L. A., & Regan, D. T. (1982). Attention, perception, and intelligence. In R. Sternberg (Ed.), *Handbook of human intelligence* (pp. 123–169). Cambridge, England: Cambridge University Press.

Cooper, L. A., & Shepard, R. N. (1973). The time required to prepare for a rotated stimulus. *Memory & Cognition, 1,* 246–250.

Cooper, L. A., & Shepard, R. N. (1984). Turning something over in the mind. *Scientific American, 251,* 106–114.

Corballis, M. C. (1988). Recognition of disoriented shapes. *Psychological Review, 95,* 115–123.

Davidson, J. E. (1986). The role of insight in giftedness. In R. J. Sternberg & J. E. Davidson (Eds.), *Conceptions of giftedness* (pp. 201–222). New York: Cambridge University Press.

de Bono, E. (1967). *New think: The use of lateral thinking in the generation of new ideas.* New York: Basic Books.

Edwards, B. (1986). *Drawing on the artist within: A guide to innovation, invention, imagination, and creativity.* New York: Simon & Schuster.

Elbow, P. (1981). *Writing without teachers.* London: Oxford University Press.

Erdelyi, M. H. (1974). A new look at the new look: Perceptual defense and vigilance. *Psychology Review, 81,* 1–25.

Farah, M. J. (1985). Psychophysical evidence for a shared representational medium for mental images and percepts. *Journal of Experimental Psychology: General, 114,* 91–103.

Farah, M. J. (1988). Is visual imagery really visual? Overlooked evidence from neuropsychology. *Psychological Review, 95,* 307–317.

Ferguson, E. S. (1977). The mind's eye: Nonverbal thought in technology. Science, 197, 827–836.

Finke, R. A. (1980). Levels of equivalence in imagery and perception. *Psychological Review, 87,* 113–132.

Finke, R. A. (1986a). Mental imagery and the visual system. *Scientific American, 254,* 88–95.

Finke, R. A. (1986b). Some consequences of visualization in pattern identification and detection. *American Journal of Psychology, 99,* 257–274.

Finke, R. A. (1989). *Principles of mental imagery.* Cambridge, MA: M.I.T. Press.

Finke, R. A., & Kurtzman, H. S. (1981). Mapping the visual field in mental imagery. *Journal of Experimental Psychology: General, 110,* 501–517.

Finke, R. A., & Pinker, S. (1982). Spontaneous imagery scanning in mental extrapolation. *Journal of Experimental Psychology: Learning, Memory, and Cognition, 8,* 142–147.

Finke, R. A., Pinker, S., & Farah, M. J. (1989). Reinterpreting visual patterns in mental imagery. *Cognitive Science, 13,* 51–78.

Finke, R. A., & Shepard, R. N. (1986). Visual functions of mental imagery. In K. R. Boff, L. Kaufman, & J. Thomas (Eds.), *Handbook of perception and human performance* (Vol. 2, Ch. 37, pp. 1–55). New York: Wiley-Interscience.

Finke, R. A., & Slayton, K. (1988). Explorations of creative visual synthesis in mental imagery. *Memory & Cognition, 16,* 252–257.

Finke, R. A., & Smith, S. M. (in preparation). Creative inspiration in mental synthesis.

Freyd, J. J. (1987). Dynamic mental representations. *Psychological Review, 94,* 427–438.

Gardner, M. (1978). *Aha! Insight.* New York: Freeman.

Gibson, E. J. (1969). *Perceptual learning and development.* New York: Appleton-Century-Crofts.

Gibson, J. J. (1966). *The senses considered as perceptual systems.* Boston: Houghton Mifflin.

Gibson, J. J. (1979). *The ecological approach to visual perception.* Boston: Houghton Mifflin.

Glushko, R. J., & Cooper, L. A. (1978). Spatial comprehension and comparison processes in verification tasks. *Cognitive Psychology, 10,* 391–421.

Hayes, J. R. (1981). *The complete problem solver.* Philadelphia: Franklin Institute Press.

Intons-Peterson, M. J. (1983). Imagery paradigms: How vulnerable are they to experimenters' expectations? *Journal of Experimental Psychology: Human Perception and Performance, 9,* 394–412.

Johansson, G. (1975). Visual motion perception. *Scientific American, 232,* 76–88.

Klopfer, D. S. (1985). Constructing mental representations of objects from successive views. *Journal of Experimental Psychology: Human Perception and Performance, 11,* 566–582.

Kosslyn, S. M. (1975). Information representation in visual images. *Cognitive Psychology, 7,* 341–370.

Kosslyn, S. M. (1976). Can imagery be distinguished from other forms of internal representation? Evidence from studies of information retrieval times. *Memory & Cognition, 4,* 291–297.

Kosslyn, S. M. (1980). *Image and mind.* Cambridge, MA: Harvard University Press.

Kosslyn, S. M., Ball, T., & Reiser, B. J. (1978). Visual images preserve metric spatial information:

Evidence from studies of image scanning. *Journal of Experimental Psychology: Human Perception and Performance, 4,* 47–60.

Kosslyn, S. M., Brunn, J. L., Cave, C. B., & Wallach, R. W. (1984). Individual differences in mental imagery ability: A computational analysis. *Cognition, 18,* 195–244.

Kosslyn, S. M., Cave, C. B., Provost, D. A., & von Gierke, S. M. (in press). Sequential processes in image generation. *Cognitive Psychology.*

Kosslyn, S. M., & Pomerantz, J. R. (1977). Imagery, propositions, and the form of internal representations. *Cognitive Psychology, 9,* 52–76.

Kosslyn, S. M., Reiser, B. J., Farah, M. J., & Fliegel, S. L. (1983). Generating visual images: Units and relations. *Journal of Experimental Psychology: General, 112,* 278–303.

Levine, M. (1987). *Effective problem solving.* Englewood Cliffs, NJ: Prentice-Hall.

Marcel, A. J. (1983). Conscious and unconscious perception: Experiments on visual masking and word recognition. *Cognitive Psychology, 15,* 197–237.

Marks, D. F. (1973). Visual imagery differences in the recall of pictures. *British Journal of Psychology, 64,* 17–24.

Marr, D., & Nishihara, H. K. (1978). Representation and recognition of the spatial organization of three-dimensional shapes. *Proceedings of the Royal Society of London, 200,* 269–294.

McKim, R. H. (1980). *Experiences in visual thinking.* Monterey, CA: Brooks/Cole.

Metcalfe, J. (1986). Feelings of knowing in memory and problem solving. *Journal of Experimental Psychology: Learning, Memory, & Cognition, 12,* 288–294.

Neblett, D. R., Finke, R. A., & Ginsburg, H. (1989). *Creative visual discoveries in physical and mental synthesis.* Manuscript submitted for publication.

Neisser, U. (1976). *Cognition and reality.* San Francisco: W. H. Freeman.

Newell, A., & Simon, H. (1972). *Human problem solving.* Englewood Cliffs, NJ: Prentice-Hall.

Nielsen, G. D., & Smith, E. E. (1973). Imaginal and verbal representations in short-term recognition of visual forms. *Journal of Experimental Psychology, 101,* 375–378.

Olton, R. M. (1979). Experimental studies of incubation: Searching for the elusive. *Journal of Creative Behavior, 13,* 9–22.

Orne, M. T. (1962). On the social psychology of the psychology experiment: With particular reference to demand characteristics and their implications. *American Psychologist, 17,* 776–783.

Osborn, A. (1953). *Applied imagination.* New York: Charles Scribner's Sons.

Pinker, S. (1980). Mental imagery and the third dimension. *Journal of Experimental Psychology: General, 109,* 354–371.

Pinker, S. (1984). Visual cognition: An introduction. *Cognition, 18,* 1–63.

Pinker, S., & Finke, R. A. (1980). Emergent two-dimensional patterns in images rotated in depth. *Journal of Experimental Psychology: Human Perception and Performance, 6,* 244–264.

Podgorny, P., & Shepard, R. N. (1978). Functional representations common to visual perception and imagination. *Journal of Experimental Psychology: Human Perception and Performance, 4,* 21–35.

Polya, G. (1957). *How to solve it.* Garden City, NY: Doubleday/Anchor.

Pylyshyn, Z. W. (1973). What the mind's eye tells the mind's brain: A critique of mental imagery. *Psychological Bulletin, 80,* 1–24.

Pylyshyn, Z. W. (1984). *Computation and cognition: Toward a foundation for cognitive science.* Cambridge, MA: M.I.T. Press.

Reed, S. K. (1974). Structural descriptions and the limitations of visual images. *Memory and Cognition, 2,* 329–336.

Rosch, E., Mervis, C. B., Gray, W. D., Johnson, D. M., & Boyes-Braem, P. (1976). Basic objects in natural categories. *Cognitive Psychology, 8,* 382–439.

Rosenthal, R. (1976). *Experimenter effects in behavioral research.* New York: Halsted Press.

Segal, S. J., & Fusella, V. (1970). Influences of imaged pictures and sounds on detection of visual and auditory signals. *Journal of Experimental Psychology, 83,* 458–464.

Shepard, R. N. (1978). Externalization of mental images and the act of creation. In B. S. Randhawa

& W. E. Coffman (Eds.), *Visual Learning, thinking, and communication* (pp. 133–189). New York: Academic Press.

Shepard, R. N. (1981). Psychophysical complementarity. In M. Kubovy & J. R. Pomerantz (Eds.), *Perceptual organization* (pp. 279–341). Hillsdale, NJ: Lawrence Erlbaum Associates.

Shepard, R. N. (1984). Ecological constraints on internal representation: Resonant kinematics of perceiving, imagining, thinking, and dreaming. *Psychological Review, 91,* 417–447.

Shepard, R. N. (1988). The imagination of the scientist. In K. Egan & D. Nadaner (Eds.), *Imagination and education* (pp. 153–185). New York: Teachers College Press.

Shepard, R. N., & Cermak, G. W. (1973). Perceptual-cognitive explorations of a toroidal set of free-form stimuli. *Cognitive Psychology, 4,* 351–377.

Shepard, R. N., & Cooper, L. A. (1982). *Mental images and their transformations.* Cambridge, MA: M.I.T. Press.

Shepard, R. N., & Feng, C. (1972). A chronometric study of mental paper folding. *Cognitive Psychology, 3,* 228–243.

Shepard, R. N., & Metzler, J. (1971). Mental rotation of three-dimensional objects. *Science, 171,* 701–703.

Slee, J. A. (1980). Individual differences in visual imagery ability and the retrieval of visual appearances. *Journal of Mental Imagery, 4,* 93–113.

Smith, E. E., & Medin, D. L. (1981). *Categories and concepts.* Cambridge, MA: Harvard University Press.

Smith, E. E., Shoben, E. J., & Rips, L. J. (1974). Structure and process in semantic memory: A featural model for demantic decisions. *Psychological Review, 81,* 214–241.

Smith, S. M., & Blankenship, S. E. (1989). Incubation effects. *Bulletin of the Psychonomic Society, 27,* 311–314.

Sternberg, R. J. (1977). *Intelligence, information processing and analogical reasoning: The componential analysis of human abilities.* Hillsdale, NJ: Lawrence Erlbaum Associates.

Sternberg, R. J. (Ed.) (1988). *The nature of creativity.* Cambridge, England: Cambridge University Press.

Thompson, A. L., & Klatzky, R. L. (1978). Studies of visual synthesis: Integration of fragments into forms. *Journal of Experimental Psychology: Human Perception and Performance, 4,* 244–263.

Torrance, E. P. (1974). *The Torrance tests of creative thinking: Norms-technical manual.* Bensenville, IL: Scholastic Testing Service.

Tversky, B. (1975). Pictorial encoding of sentences in sentence-picture comparison. *Quarterly Journal of Experimental Psychology, 27,* 405–410.

Weisberg, R. W. (1986). *Creativity, genius and other myths.* New York: Freeman.

Wickelgren, W. A. (1974). *How to solve problems.* San Francisco: Freeman.

Author Index

Subject Index

emergent patterns in, 7, 9–18, 27–28, 32, 60, 125, 168, 171

number of parts in, 9, 21–22, 32, 40, 103, 142, 174

preparation time in, 21

vs. physical synthesis, 31–33

strategies for, 27, 32, 37, 58, 83, 140, 167

complexity of parts in, 9, 23, 40

in three dimensions, 40, 174

Mental transformations. *See also* Mental imagery; Mental rotation; Preinventive forms, manipulation of

accuracy of, 12–13, 15–17

recognition of patterns following, 12–18, 125, 171

of shape, 22, 40

of size, 22, 40

N

Necker cube, 8–9

Nondirective thinking, 3

P

Patterns, creative. *See also* Concepts, creative; Inventions, creative

constraints on, 21–22

inspiration for, 23, 33–36, 167

parts used in, 22–23, 32, 34

predictions of, 24–25, 27–29, 36–37

ratings of, 24

uniqueness of, 29–31

Practice effects, 29, 31, 45, 67, 88, 147, 167, 172

Preinventive forms. *See also* Concepts, creative; Inventions, creative; Mental images; Problem solving, using preinventive forms

in children's drawings, 175

commitment to, 87, 89, 146, 167, 173–174

construction of, 83–85, 89, 167, 171–174

illusion of intentionality in, 3, 107

interpretation of, 3, 18, 83–85, 87, 89, 106, 109–111, 118, 125, 129, 140, 144–145, 162, 165, 167–170, 172–174

"magical" quality of, 106–107

manipulation of, 110–111, 118, 125, 140, 171, 174

number of parts in, 103, 174

persistence of, 84, 110, 172

ratings of, 85, 87

refinement of, 88, 110, 172

reinterpretation of, 134, 140

selection of, 84, 134, 174–175

types of, 86, 89–105, 110–140, 142–143, 147–164, 174

as universal solutions, 61, 108, 170, 174

usefulness of, 85, 87–89, 141, 162, 165, 167, 169, 171–173

as visual metaphors. 141

Principles of imagery, 171

Problem solving

using brainstorming, 108

expertise in, 165, 173

functional fixedness in, 60

general strategies for, 4, 170

incubation in, 169

using means-end analysis, 169–170

predicting success on, 37

using preinventive forms, 165, 168–170

by working backwards, 170

Propositions, 18–19

R

Reader participation

for creative concepts, 157–158

for creative inventions, 58–59

for creative patterns, 25–27

for preinventive forms, 103, 106–107

for restrictive inventions, 80

for visual discoveries, 10, 12–15

Reasoning. *See* Problem solvinig

Recognition, visual, 7–18, 21–32, 34, 36–37, 39, 60, 109, 125, 134, 169, 171. *See also* Mental imagery; Mental synthesis; Mental transformations

S

Schema, 147

Special relativity, 2

Superordinate categories, 42, 64–65